"One compelling lesson evident i
that the scars of childhood bullyir
a lifetime. Another is that even o
counselor, or especially in her case a
make all the difference in rescuing and revitalizing that wounded
child and child-within. In an era of relentless headlines of anxiety
and despair, *The Lifesaving Church* arrives on the scene as a welcome—
and welcoming—witness to perseverance and hope."
— Robert C. Dykstra, professor, Princeton Theological Seminary

"*The Lifesaving Church* is a powerful book about suicide prevention
that every church leader needs to read. Through compelling and
courageous storytelling, followed by practical steps that you can do
today, this book is a guide that will help churches fulfill their mission
to save lives."
— Sarah Griffith Lund, First Congregational Church of Indianapolis
  and author of *Blessed Are the Crazy*

"Keefe has offered us a fearless telling of her own story of struggle
and hope, of pain and healing, and of betrayal and redemption.
She has used her experiences of suicidal thoughts (and an attempt),
a persistent eating disorder, and a deep 'psycheache' to weave a
theology of the Church and its purpose of saving lives. Her story
serves as both a spiritual and practical guide to congregations as they
seek to be a healing and hopeful presence to all they serve, especially
those struggling with suicide, addictions, and a sense of separation
from God, neighbor, and self. The book includes practical suggestions
as well as multiple resources in the appendices."
— Christie Cozad Neuger, professor emerita, Brite Divinity School.

"Keefe courageously tells her story of pain and woundedness and the
miracle of transformation that she found in her faith community.
This is not just her story. She provides several concrete suggestions for
mental health ministry and congregational care. She offers options for
preventing and responding to suicide that move beyond platitudes or
clichés. She is witness to Christ's promise that exposing her wounds
to her faith community, the Body of Christ, will lead to redemption.
Once redeemed, Keefe's pain became wisdom. She has been able to
use her personal flaws as tools to understand and offer healing and
compassionate space to others."
— David W. McMillan, clinical and community psychologist

"This book weaves the power of Keefe's personal story with theological and psychological wisdom. Suicidal behavior, self-harm, eating disorder, depression, and adverse (abusive and neglected) childhood experiences are realities that connect with her experience of the embodied love of God. This book breaks the silence with her honesty and the depth of her faithfulness and guides faith communities to embody the unconditional love of the divine. 'God is not a fan of suicide,' is a wallop of grace that engages us in the conversation."

— Alan Johnson, United Church of Christ Mental Health Network

"Keefe offers a timely and relevant introduction to what it means to be mindful and attentive to the realities of suicide in our midst. This is an aspect of ministry that has certainly been under addressed. She shares her personal journey, which has involved suicidal realities as well as gender realities, to alert communities of faith to their critical role in responding to people who may be overlooked in their day-to-day living. Her brave revelations of her journey toward healing can be a needed inspiration to those who think they are alone in their life situations. Her voice throughout her narration is particularly powerful. She weaves personal reflections with theological insights to provide hope for those struggling with similar issues. Because she speaks from personal experience, her confession is compelling and inspiring for others who may be dealing with all too similar situations. Particularly helpful are her appendices, which give practical instruction for those dealing with issues of suicide. Her wisdom is instructive for counseling families and friends affected by suicidal relations. Also helpful are her keen insights into the faith and psychological dynamics that are a part of suicidal realities."

— Sharon Thornton, professor emerita, Andover Newton Theological School and author of *Broken Yet Beloved*

"At last, a healthy, soul-stirring resource for starting a conversation about suicide in the church! Through a courageous personal testimony, Keefe reminds us that no one is outside of God's reach, and calls the church to return to the heart of its DNA as an institution of love and radical acceptance. Keefe proves that vulnerability and raw truth telling, coupled with professional insight and genuine unconditional love, is our only hope if we truly are to become *The Lifesaving Church*."

— Angela Whitenhill, Mental Health Initiative manager, National Benevolent Association (Christian Church/Disciples of Christ)

THE LIFESAVING CHURCH

FAITH COMMUNITIES AND SUICIDE PREVENTION

RACHAEL A. KEEFE

chalice
press

Saint Louis, Missouri

An imprint of Christian Board of Publication

Cover design: Jesse Turri
Cover art: Photograph copyright ©2018 by Chalice Press.

ChalicePress.com

Print ISBN: 9780827221826
EPUB: 9780827221833   EPDF: 9780827221840

Printed in the United States of America

Contents

*To the Rev. John Hall, without whom my story could not be told.
Words are insufficient to express my gratitude for the decades of
listening, caring, mentoring, and friendship that
grew out of my bleakest moments.*

Acknowledgments

If you have touched my life with love and grace, I'm grateful. I think of the members of the Federated Church of Hyannis back in the 1980s, teachers, professors, therapists, and friends who have shared the journey; there are no words to sufficiently express my gratitude for all of you. With a book like this one, it is impossible to thank all those who contributed in one way or another. I feel as if I'd have to name everyone I've ever known, and I would inevitably leave someone significant out. To avoid that, those listed here are people who directly participated in the writing process.

Sarah Lund, who made me realize the time had come to tell my story.

The folks of Living Table United Church of Christ, who allowed me to take a week away to begin the writing process, and offered their support in the ongoing endeavor.

The women at Holy Wisdom Monastery in Middleton, Wisconsin, for the hospitality and welcome into sacred community while I began writing.

Wendy Stoll, Timothy Thomas, and John Hall for reading the first draft and encouraging me to keep going.

All the folks at Chalice Press who made this book feel like a collaborative adventure—Brad Lyons, Deborah Arca, Ulrike Guthrie, Gail Stobaugh, KJ Reynolds, and anyone else with whom I didn't have direct contact.

The United Church of Christ Mental Health Network, who encouraged me to share my knowledge and experiences in ways that led me to develop my theological approach to suicidality.

My colleagues, my wife's colleagues, and the members of RevGalBlogPals who shared their questions around suicide prevention, intervention, and postvention. Their responses helped shape the content of this book.

And, as always, my wife, Erika Sanborne, without whose support, companioning, and love I could not have written this book.

Preface

This isn't a book about suicide so much as it is about suicide prevention. It's about what can happen when the Church, the Body of Christ, actually embodies the love of Christ and saves lives. This book is also more than that. It is my story, my remembering of my own experiences of suicidality, suicidal behaviors, and romancing of death. The details of this story are now filtered through my decades of experience as a pastor, as well as my years as a therapist and a clinical chaplain. Life and ministry have shaped and reshaped my self-understanding and have, no doubt, shifted things in my memory as I have grown more fully into myself.

I don't write this book because I think I have all the answers. I write to engage in conversation with you. Suicide seems to be one of the last taboos of the church. It makes most of us anxious when someone talks about suicide. Requests for prayers for a loved one who is hospitalized for suicidal behavior are nearly whispered—if they are spoken out loud at all. People often shy away from survivors of suicide loss because they are uncomfortable and don't know what to say. And those who might want prayers—let alone tangible, embodied care for their own struggles with suicidality—often don't dare to ask. There's so much silence around suicide in the church that it is quite literally killing us, though we are supposed to be a people of abundant life.

The church is a community bound together for life through the love of Christ. It is the Body of Christ, a whole, rather than separate individuals. When describing the struggle of individuals within the church, I frequently say, "As with one, so with all." If one member of the church is mentally ill, the Body of Christ is mentally ill. If one member is disabled, the Body of Christ is disabled. If one member has cancer, the Body of Christ has cancer...and so on, down the line...including suicidality. If one member of the church is suicidal, then the Body of Christ is suicidal, hence my chapter titles: "The Body of Christ Is Suicidal," "The Body of Christ Holds Secrets and Shame," "The Body of Christ Is Resilient," "The Body of Christ Is Broken and Whole," "The Body of Christ Is a Lifesaver," and so forth.

Jesus asks us to carry one another's burdens. How better to do this than to assume responsibility for healing the Body of Christ?

Chapter 1

The Body of Christ Is Suicidal

My God, my God why have you forsaken me?
Why are you so far from helping me, from the
words of my groaning? —Psalm 22:1

On February 13, 1983, when I was 15 I tried to kill myself. It was the next day before anyone knew that I had swallowed a potentially lethal combination of medications. Later, people assumed that my actions were mere adolescent drama—perhaps because I had no date for Valentine's Day, or had broken up with a boy, or the usual things said to minimize adolescent pain. It wasn't any of these things. No, it wasn't dating drama that made me want to die. It was the *rest* of my life.

My problem was not unusual. I lived in a very unhappy household and I saw no way out. My mother had her own struggles and she simply did not know what to do with a sensitive child. Her motto was "No Blood, No Tears," and I was a child who cried very easily. By the time I was 15, though, I had learned not to cry so much, if at all. And I had begun to fear that if I started crying I would never stop, for the pain I was carrying within me was bigger than everything else in my experience. Given that this pain was also a secret, then my desire to die, to end the pain, was no surprise to me. In seventh grade, I had gotten into a physical fight with another student. Everyone was shocked because I was the model student: I never missed a day of school, I completed all of my assignments, and I never caused any problems. That day, in seventh grade art class, I finally acted on my feelings. I was always being picked on, made fun of, and bullied. Unlike most students, I liked art class and I was pretty good at it. Then one kid said something mocking me to another kid and, without thinking, I walked up to him and shoved him. He responded by punching me in the face. That was it. I was hurt, and horrified by what I had done.

After that I was referred to the guidance counselor. I told her about how my mother drank from Thanksgiving until New Year's, and about the hours I spent alone with my older brother who was abusive. I told her how I essentially had no friends in school and how everyone teased me about my clothes, the way I looked, and how weird I was. After meeting with the guidance counselor a few times and trying to tell her about all the pain in my young life, she essentially told me I had PMS and should pay more attention to my feelings around "that time of the month." She left me feeling more guilty and ashamed than I had been before I met with her. It was several years before I tried to tell anyone else what was happening in my life.

The shame that took hold of me in my middle-school years grew stronger in high school. On the outside, I did everything I was supposed to do. I went to school and did well. I was active in church. I had a steady babysitting job. I made a few friends. The rest of it, I kept to myself. I pretended that none of my home life was real. I figured that the years my brother tormented me by locking me in the closet or in the basement "with the spiders" or out in the snow barefoot or the countless other things he would do for his own amusement weren't real if I didn't acknowledge them. The ways in which my mother made me feel stupid, ugly, and unwanted didn't matter if I got As in school and no one else knew what my life at home was like. Somehow, I started to believe that if I didn't say something out loud, it did not exist.

I played this game of pretend with myself until my sophomore year of high school. I desperately wanted to be in the drama club.

In my freshman year, I had a crush on a boy who was one of the stars of the club, and I determined that I would get to be in it, too. In my sophomore year I managed to get a part in the fall musical even though I truly could not sing or dance. I quit my regular babysitting job so I could be in the play. I stayed after school to work on the sets and that would meld into evening practice. It wasn't long before I made the strange discovery that I did not need to eat.

I'd long ago stopped eating much, if anything, for breakfast. By middle school, I had stopped eating lunch in school and would just buy milk. In elementary school, my mother packed me a lunch—which I did eat, without thinking much about it. However, in fifth grade I started to be aware that I was bigger than my classmates. To my ten-year-old brain, being bigger, weighing more, meant that I was fat. This sense of being fat increased over the next few years. So as my eating habits were changed by peer influences, my underlying perception of being fat became much more dominant. I stopped eating lunch in sixth grade, which didn't seem problematic to me. We qualified for reduced lunch, which meant that I bought lunch at school but was made fun of for eating the school food. The simplest course of action was to stop eating, since I already thought I was fat. In ninth grade, I would eat something at lunch, but not exactly a meal. When my schedule changed and I didn't know anyone who shared my lunch period, I just went to the library instead of the cafeteria. By the time I got to tenth grade, I seldom ate breakfast and never ate lunch. I would eat cookies while babysitting and I would eat dinner. However, when I had drama club, I didn't even have to eat dinner. Sometimes I would go with a friend and get a sandwich or a donut, but there were often days on which I would eat nothing at all.

It wasn't long before people noticed that I had lost some weight. Many would tell me how great I looked, how grown up. The funny thing is that I was never overweight, and people had already thought I was four or five years older than I was. But it didn't matter. I liked the power I felt over my body. I liked the feeling of control. The thought of disappearing was one that pleased me. Until the fear and guilt set in.

When the play ended and I had to return to my "normal" life, I discovered that I had become very afraid to eat. But I also had the need to hide my internal struggle. As a result, when I had to eat dinner with my mother, I would. And then I would vomit. Then I would feel ashamed. I knew that what I was doing was wrong, but I could not stop it. I loved the sense of power and control over my body while I knew, with startling certainty, that starving myself and purging was very wrong. Somehow, though, what I thought of as control over my body had suddenly taken control of me. I was powerless to stop engaging in the cycle of starvation, binging, and purging.

Now we get to February 13, 1983. I was miserable. I felt trapped. Everything seemed at a distance. I lived in a fog in which nothing felt real except the pain I was in. Some days I wasn't even sure how real that was. It was a Sunday afternoon. I had come home from church and determined yet again that I would stop starving, or eating and purging. So I ate what was probably a normal meal but seemed overwhelming to me. And then I purged. When I opened the bathroom closet to get a towel, I saw all the medication bottles. There weren't a lot of them and I didn't know what they all were and I didn't know which were current and which were not. I just took several from each bottle. I didn't want to take all of any of them because I didn't want anyone to know what I had done before I died.

Then I went through the rest of the day as usual, waiting for something to happen. Nothing did. I'm sure I went to youth group that night and came home to finish my homework. Then I went to bed feeling really sad and angry because I couldn't even kill myself right. I was worthless. I couldn't eat. I couldn't not eat. I couldn't even die. Maybe God wanted me to suffer...

I woke up the next morning, earlier than my alarm. I was going to be sick. I managed to get down the stairs to the bathroom, even though everything was distorted. The walls were at weird angles and my arms and legs were ten feet long and everything was moving. I somehow managed to get to the bathroom to throw up but there was nothing in my stomach. The last thing I remember is thinking I should tell my mother that I was too sick to go to school.

The next thing I knew, I was in the emergency room at the local hospital. Doctors and nurses were yelling at me, asking me what I had taken and where I had gotten it. I had a vague notion that they thought I'd overdosed on illegal drugs. I wanted to escape back into the darkness, back where it was quiet and I didn't have to face the anxious, angry faces hovering around me. (If you or someone you know is feeling like this, see Appendix D: "Resources for Those Struggling with Suicidality.")

Saving Church

The day I tried to kill myself was a turning point. It marked the end of my passive acceptance of pain. As difficult and as complicated as it was, I began the journey of recovery the week I spent in the hospital following my overdose. It was by no means a smooth or easy path, and it was not short: it has taken me a lifetime to undo the lessons of my childhood. However, from that day on, I knew that I was not walking the path alone.

John, who was the associate pastor of the Federated Church of Hyannis, my childhood church, came to visit me in the emergency room. He came that first day and he kept coming back. I felt no judgment from him. He wanted to help. He listened and did not leave me alone. Even after I was discharged, he came to see me regularly. Somewhere along the way, I promised that I would not try to kill myself again, a promise I kept with some difficulty.

For years I have said that John saved my life. He was the first person who embodied Christ's love for me. He didn't want anything from me except, perhaps, that I not die. He cared without the expectation that I would give him anything or do anything for him. There was no condition on his showing up. I needed that more than he probably knew, certainly more than I knew.

It wasn't John alone who saved my life, though: it was the whole congregation. I had been going to the church since I was in third grade. However, it was only after the overdose that I began to feel a real sense of caring from the congregation. Before that, I was accepted, sure. I was the kid who was dropped off early for Sunday school and worship, and picked up late. The same for choir practice and youth group. I was always dropped off early and picked up late, so much so that it became easier for the youth leaders to drive me home than to wait for my mother to come and get me.

My mother wasn't a fan of church. She had been raised Catholic and held a lot of anger toward the church for reasons she never chose to share with me. She thought religion was a "crutch for weak people." On the other hand, she didn't see how she could say no when her eight-year-old daughter asked to go. In the mid-1970s on Cape Cod, most kids still went to church, catechism classes, or Hebrew school. I stood out enough for being taller, wearing handmade clothes, needing glasses, having divorced parents, and so many other things. I thought church would make me normal, or at least enough like my classmates that life would be easier.

At first, I went to church with my mother's friend who had two children around my age. They would pick me up and take me to church for Sunday school and children's choir. After a while, they moved and started attending another church, so my mother begrudgingly drove me. I made friends and people accepted my presence. I liked church. My mother did not, but she had enough Catholicism in her that she couldn't say no to my going. She did make it a point on many occasions to tell me just how foolish she thought my belief in God and my desire for religion were. She didn't realize that church was the only safe place for me. I didn't have to protect myself there. I didn't have to hide so much there. I could ask questions and think that maybe there was a God who cared, if not about me, then about the wider world.

Reflecting on all of this now, the biblical character Nicodemus comes to mind (Jn. 3). He snuck out to talk with Jesus under the cover of darkness. He wanted what Jesus was offering. He wanted the Light so much that he was willing to risk ridicule by his colleagues in order to find out what he needed to do. Of course, Jesus didn't answer his question in a way that made sense to Nicodemus. Nicodemus did not understand what Jesus meant by a person needing to be born anew, or born from above, or born again. He probably felt that he should know what Jesus was talking about in that moment, but he didn't. I think he did later, though, because he didn't give up: Nicodemus stood up for Jesus against the rest of the Pharisees (Jn. 7:50–51). Later, he helped Joseph of Arimathea prepare Jesus' body for the tomb (Jn. 19:38–40). Nicodemus found what he needed.

As an adolescent, I needed the new life about which Jesus spoke to Nicodemus that dark night. The quest to be normal, like everyone else, was what had drawn me to the church. That the church held the power of life—the power to save lives, my own and others'—took me years to discover. John came to see me in the emergency room because I was a child of the church. He kept coming to see me because he had hope for me. I went to the church under the cover of the darkness of my childhood. I was met with Light.

John freely offered his presence and support, as did others. The congregation rallied to support me in the days, weeks, months, and years that followed. When I was hospitalized for two months for eating disorder treatment, they sent cards and gifts and welcomed me when I was home on weekend passes. When John moved to another church, the congregation's care for me did not stop. The congregation showed me that I had value, that they wanted me there, and that I mattered. Of course, it took me years to claim this truth, but that did not change what they did. Eventually, I accepted the love they freely offered.

Without knowing it, this congregation gave me an understanding of church at its very best. They saved me. I didn't know it then, but the lessons of acceptance, love, and value that I learned in that congregation were going to sustain me through some very challenging times many years later. The Federated Church of Hyannis, its members and clergy, literally and spiritually saved my life. I didn't learn much in the way of theology and doctrine there, I didn't have any kind of dramatic conversion experience, but they embodied Christ's love for me at a time when it really mattered.

When I was in college, the Christian fellowship group with which I was involved for a while often asked people, "When were you saved?" I made up an answer because I didn't think I had actually been saved from anything or for anything. They were looking for a Damascus Road (Acts 9:1–19) kind of conversion experience. The truth was, I was saved when an ordinary congregation on Cape Cod embodied Christian love in a way that changed my life. The change was gradual, for sure, but no less transformative for that.

Psychache

I often describe my teenage years as a period of romancing death. I didn't necessarily want to die as much as I wanted the pain to end. I had a very romantic notion of death as being a peaceful escape from everything I could not face. If I could have imagined another way to rid myself of pain, I don't think I would have courted death quite as long. I was trapped, though, and had no conception that life wouldn't always be so hard or so painful.

Even before I was caught in the torment of an eating disorder, I described myself as living in a box. It was a two-way mirror box. I could see out but people looking at me saw mostly what they wanted to see. Rarely would I feel as if someone could actually see that I was trapped in my pain. I truly felt I was confined there, bound in chains with no hope of release. My feelings were a mystery to me and I couldn't articulate them. I felt all caged up with no way out. This is how I described my life at 16.

I lived with a numbness to everything except despair. Very seldom did other emotions touch me. When they did, I didn't trust them very much. My feelings, my responses to situations were almost always invalidated. I remember an afternoon when I was maybe 11 and home alone with my brother Colin, who was two years older. He made me go down to the basement for something, knowing that I was afraid of the spiders that seemed to proliferate down there. There was a light switch on the wall at the top of the stairs and then other lights that had pull strings, most of which I couldn't reach. There were small windows that didn't let much light in. As soon as I got to the bottom of the stairs, Colin turned the light off and locked the basement door. He said he would let me in the house if I went out the bulkhead doors. I was terrified of the dark, cobweb-filled steps that led up to those metal doors. They were also heavy and hard for me to open. I did get them open and get out to the backyard. Of course, he wouldn't let me in the back door and had locked that, too. The gate to the front of the house was padlocked and I didn't have the key with me. He told me to climb over the fence and he would let me in the front door. I was afraid of heights and didn't have shoes on. I went to climb up the chain link and he met me with the water hose. Now I was both wet and frustrated. He told me to go climb out on the stockade side of the fence. I couldn't. I could climb up, but there was no way to climb down. I remember just standing there at the corner of the fence and screaming, a shriek of pure frustration.

The neighbor came out and told me that I shouldn't scream like that if nothing was wrong. My brother laughed. I learned not to make any more noise because it achieved nothing. His torment of me usually left no marks, and even when it did, no one noticed. All the anger and frustration that built up during the years he made my life miserable had no outlet. I learned that I did not matter. My mother didn't believe I should cry if I wasn't bleeding and the neighbor didn't think I should scream if nothing visible was wrong. I retreated into depression and silence.

A few years ago, I was at a conference where I heard a paper presented on *"psychache."* Even though I had been an outpatient therapist and a clinical chaplain at a psychiatric hospital, this was a new term for me. *Psychache,* a term coined by Edwin Shneidman,[1] describes intense, unbearable psychological pain that results from significant unmet psychological needs. When left unresolved, psychache leads to suicide, or at least suicidal thoughts or behaviors. When I first heard this term, it shifted my understanding of myself and the patients with whom I worked.

To my knowledge, Shneidman doesn't say anything about spiritual needs when he refers to psychache. However, for me this term encompasses more than depression or PTSD or other diagnoses a suicidal person might receive. It speaks to the need to love and be loved and to belong somewhere with someone. These are psychological needs that, when unmet, lead to maladaptive behaviors. They are also spiritual needs that, when unmet, lead to incredible pain, pain that is overwhelming and unspeakable and unbreakable. Psychache truly feels insurmountable. It can't be surgically cut out, starved out, purged out, run out, drowned out, smoked out, or snorted out. It's the kind of pain that drives

---

1 Edward Shneidman, *Suicide as Psychache* (Lanham, Md.: Jason Aronson, Inc., 1995).

a person to self-destruction by any means at hand, sometimes by multiple means. Psychache is, as Shneidman points out, *pain*, not illness. It can't be cured, but it can be healed.

In seminary, I had the privilege of studying with Dr. James Loder.[2] He put spiritual development and faith formation alongside psychological development. He used the works of Erik Erikson and Jean Piaget to lay a foundation for spiritual development. He spoke about "faith saving us from the void." As Loder described it, the void is the place of emptiness, nothingness, longing—or, in other words, the place where God is not. The void, to my understanding, is the birthplace of psychache. As an infant grows, she needs affirmation and confirmation that she is not alone in the world and there are others who will meet her needs. When those basic needs aren't met, a void develops in her and the ache begins.

The love and care I received as a child were wholly inadequate and very sporadic. My mother was often unavailable physically or emotionally. My father visited on Sundays and could not be trusted. He was and is an alcoholic and a pathological liar. I never knew what, if anything, he said was true. What I knew was that what I wanted or needed didn't matter. I had to accept what was offered. My father took me to R-rated movies when I was nine or ten. My mother gave me *Lady Chatterly's Lover*[3] to read when I was 11. When it came to birthdays or Christmas, I never ever got what I asked for and actually wanted or needed. In addition to learning not to trust myself, I learned not to trust anyone else.

When I was about four years old, my brother set fire to the living room carpet. He had found a book of matches and wanted to know how they worked. We'd seen our parents light cigarettes countless times. So Colin went into the living room and managed

---

2 The book for which Loder was best known at the time I studied with him is *The Transforming Moment* (Colorado Springs: Helmers and Howard, 1989). This book and the classes I had with Dr. Loder had a significant influence on the development of my theology and my understanding of faith formation.

3 This book by D. H. Lawrence was first published in 1928. It is the story of a woman who is lonely and unhappy in her marriage. It chronicles her affair with the game keeper who works on her husband's estate. The book, while a beautiful, lyrical novel, is not appropriate for a child, as it is sexually explicit.

to light a match and drop it onto the shag carpeting. I remember pouring a cup of water on the small flame. When our parents saw the burn in the carpet, they were angry and demanded to know who had done it. They asked us both in turn if we were responsible. I said that I didn't do it. Colin, of course, said that he didn't do it. They decided to punish us both. They whipped us with the leather dog leash. I learned that even telling the truth couldn't protect me from guilt and shame and punishment.

As the years went on, experiences of inadequacy and pain layered one on top of another until I believed that all I was was pain. I really thought that it would never get any better. I had run out of ways of coping with the overwhelming bleakness. What hope could I have had in my family? Death would have been a welcome release, I thought. Not even God seemed big enough to overcome what I perceived as a thick and heavy fog that separated me from everyone and everything.

Loder taught me the language of faith and the possibility of a joyful life in the Spirit. Many years later, at an American Psychological Association Division 36 (Society for the Psychology of Religion) conference, I learned the word for the pain I had lived with. Yes, I was depressed. Yes, I had PTSD. Yes, I had an eating disorder. However, none of those described my pain. *Before* all those things manifested, there was psychache, the overwhelming pain of feeling unwanted, dismissed, ignored, rejected, bullied, and abused.

What Your Congregation Can Do Now:

- Learn the signs that indicate a person is at risk for suicide. (See Appendix A: "Signs of Suicide Risk.)

- Respond to mental health crises the same way the congregation responds to any other health crisis — by visiting the person in the hospital or at home, by bringing food, by offering help and support, and with specific prayers. (See Appendix G: Prayers.)

- Use the resources of your denomination to develop a mental health ministry in your congregation. For example, the Mental Health Network of the United Church of Christ has

Chapter 2

The Body of Christ
Holds Secrets and Shame

Where can I go from your spirit?
Or where can I flee from your presence?
If I ascend to heaven, you are there;
if I make my bed in Sheol, you are there.

—Psalm 139:7–8

By the time I overdosed, I was already ensnared in an eating disorder. I would avoid eating whenever possible; and when it wasn't possible, I would eat reluctantly and then purge. It took my mother a while to notice, but not very long. A few days before I ODed, Karen Carpenter died from complications of anorexia. Suddenly, it seemed, everyone knew what an eating disorder was. A therapist, teachers, pastors, and even my mother encouraged me to read more about it. I read *The Best Little Girl in the World*[1] and *Starving for Attention*,[2] and I learned not so much about anorexia

---

1 Steven Levenkron, *The Best Little Girl in the World* (Chicago: Contemporary Books, 1978). While this is a novel, it tells the very real struggles of those who live with anorexia. I learned about counting calories and exercising to the extreme through reading this book.

2 Cherry Boone O'Neil, *Starving for Attention* (New York: Continuum, 1982). This is the biography of Pat Boone's daughter, Cherry, in which she vividly describes her struggle with an eating disorder. Reading this book taught me how to use laxatives as another form of purging.

and what causes it, but how to do it better. In the days before the Internet, these books gave me ideas about exercise, calorie counting, and laxatives. As my behaviors worsened, so did my sense of shame.

I couldn't actually talk about these things. I would deny counting calories. No one knew that I was obsessed with the number 100. In school, it was a sign of perfection. Then it became the number of calories any given food I could eat could contain. Then it became the number of calories I could eat in a day without purging. It also became the number of sit-ups, jumping jacks, crunches, leg lifts, and the like that I would do at a time, several times a day. But my secret desire was to weigh 100 pounds. At 5'7" with a truly large bone structure, that was a bad idea. My pre-eating disorder weight was 140 pounds and I was not at all fat.

My therapist would ask about all these things and I wouldn't answer. John would try to get me to talk about my feelings and I couldn't answer. Each time I knew he was coming to see me, I would promise myself that I would tell him something about my fears and some of the things that had happened to me. Then he would get there and ask his questions, and my answers would get stuck in my throat. When I was unable to speak, the harder I tried to break the silence, the further away from myself I seemed to be. It would often feel as if I was floating far above the silence, screaming at myself to open my mouth and let some of the pain out. As much as I wanted to use my voice, I could not. I would disappear into the silence.

By the time I was hospitalized on June 10, 1983, I weighed 112 pounds and lived with a fear of eating and drinking. I also lived with a deep sense of shame. I knew that what I was doing to myself was wrong. I thought that even God would be angry at everything I was doing to myself in an effort to become perfect. On the other hand, I really believed that if I weighed 100 pounds I would be perfect and I would be seen and loved and wanted.

The treatment I received at Boston Children's Hospital was fine for what it was. I was so hopeful when I went. I thought that if I did everything that was asked of me, I would get better. And I tried to do everything they asked. I sat through horrible family meetings with my parents, who had been divorced for more than a decade. I got through these by telling myself how much worse it would be if my brother were there, too, instead of his being away for basic training in the Marines. I ate what I was supposed to. I drank what they told me to drink—once they found out that I hadn't been drinking anything. I listened to my mother's angry words because she thought everyone blamed her for my eating disorder. I tried to be honest when asked about my feelings. I created the illusion of compliance and they changed my diagnosis to depression. I was too good to have a real eating disorder.

After that, I remember feeling so angry at myself that I took my little embroidery scissors (that I was allowed to keep because needle work was a "positive coping skill") and tried to cut my wrists with them. My intent wasn't to die, although I thought I'd be okay with that. Rather, it was to show someone how much I hurt. My words were inadequate or nonexistent so I thought blood would show them something. Those scissors were so blunt that I was barely able to scratch my wrist. No one noticed. And, as usual, I said nothing.

Generally speaking, though, I felt safe while I was in the hospital. The rules and expectations were clear there. I didn't have to guess what anyone wanted from me and I had no fear of being physically injured. I did manage to eat meals and snacks and continue to lose weight. I stopped purging for the most part. I made friends with some of the other girls. In later years when my friends talked about summer camp experiences, I thought about my time in the hospital. It was the most "normal" part of my adolescence.

Unfortunately, I honestly didn't get any better during those two months. No one really believed you could recover from an eating disorder in those days. The best that could be hoped for was managing the behaviors. I did that fairly well while in the hospital. Out in the world was another story.

Around the time I was being prepared for discharge, my mother's best friend became suddenly and critically ill. She was dying from what was described to me as a "rare blood disease" while I was hospitalized for something I was deliberately doing to myself. I felt so guilty. My mother had to make repeated trips to Boston for me, and now for her friend. My mother let me know how she felt about that, too. She was angry at me. She was scared for her friend also, but at 16 I thought all those ugly feelings she had were really directed at me.

The day after I was discharged, I had to take care of my mother's friend's daughter, Jenny. Jenny was 13, and no one had told her that her mother was dying. I didn't think that was right and there was nothing I could do about it. Jenny didn't find me much fun and went to play with the girls next door. I proceeded to binge and purge as if I hadn't just spent two months learning how not to do that.

On top of all this, as I'd mentioned earlier, John had accepted a call to a church in Pennsylvania. He promised that we would stay in touch and he assured me that his leaving had nothing to do with me. I thought the latter was weird because I couldn't imagine that I had that kind of power in anyone's life. Of course, his choices to move didn't have anything to do with me! However, I do remember thinking that if he truly cared as much as he said he did, he wouldn't have left. Even then, I didn't actually believe that. I just didn't want him to go. More accurately, I wanted him to go and take me with him.

Thus began my junior year in high school. The only good thing about that year was that it was my last in high school. All the psychological testing at the hospital had revealed that I was academically well beyond high school. When I was admitted, I remember my mother telling the social worker that I worried about grades too much. She recounted how there was one biology test over which I had become particularly distraught. What she didn't know was that my frustration was about not being able to figure out beforehand what was going to be on the test, not about the test itself. My mother also described how much work I would put into projects, sometimes staying up late into the night to get them done. What she didn't know is that I had come to think of staying up late at night as a way of burning more calories. I would often tell her that I had to work on a project even when I'd already finished it. After the testing, though, the social worker told my mother that if I wasn't getting all As it was because I was not trying and I was likely bored.

This is why my mother finally consented to let me graduate early, something for which I had been asking since the beginning of my freshman year. I think most people thought I got better that year. I had a new therapist and I met with the senior pastor regularly after John left. I was pretty content to let people think I was fine. I kept my weight between 102 and 105 pounds because I was told that I would have to go back to the hospital if my weight went below 102. It was one thing to spend the summer in the hospital, it would have been another to be there during the school year. I wanted to graduate so I could leave home. Besides, my mother had told me on the drive home from the hospital that if I ever went back, I would be going alone. Given how alone I already felt, her words terrified me.

The Word of Life

It was during my last year of high school that I decided I wanted to go into the ministry. In part, I wanted to be like John. I also had a sense of needing to "pay back" all that the church had done for me. This reasoning was a bit misguided, but the call was real nonetheless.

When I was about nine, I had read a book called *Missionary Stories*. I don't know who wrote it but I can still picture the cover. It was a thin paperback with a picture of a red boat on a river with an exotic-looking jungle in the background. It contained several short stories about different people's experiences as missionaries in various countries in Africa during the 1920s and 1930s. I was captivated by the accounts of building schools, digging wells, translating the Bible into local dialects, providing medical care, and other such activities. I loved that little book. I read it several times before I told my mother that I wanted to be a missionary when I grew up. Her response was, "Over my dead body." I didn't talk to her about it after that. I let her think that I wanted to be a special education teacher instead.

My sense of call was born in those dark days of my childhood. My grandmother, who always identified herself as "Irish Catholic," sent Bible stories as Christmas gifts early on in our lives in hopes of saving her "heathen" grandchildren. These were picture books accompanied by 45 rpm records with Burl Ives narrating the stories—stories about Noah, Jonah, Joseph and his robe of many colors, and several others. I fell in love with these stories and they, no doubt, fueled my desire to go to church. I was fascinated by the idea of a God who created, loved, and redeemed the whole world. I wanted that God to be my Father and I wanted him to love me.

In my innocence, I didn't know that God already loved me and that it was the Holy Spirit who was pulling me toward church. It was years before I understood that there is a reason that Jesus is the Word become flesh. As I became more able to speak my truth out loud, usually in the safety of a therapist's or spiritual director's office, I started to grasp the power of words and the Word. Jesus broke God's perceived silence in the world. He spoke against those in power and acted on behalf of the forgotten and unwanted ones. The Word that created all that is became the Word that saves humanity from itself. This is the Word that the church must speak out loud because lives are still at risk of suicide or being lost in the deadening fog of psychache today.

Today's church seems to have forgotten its power. On the progressive side, we have worked so hard to be politically correct, to not assert our faith as being better than another, that we have inadvertently left behind the potency of the gospel. On the other hand, more conservative churches have favored doctrine and dogma nearly to the point of squeezing the life out of the Spirit. In both cases, we tend to neglect the pain of the person standing in our doorway in favor of the "right" way of doing things, according to whatever traditions a particular congregation has adopted and made sacrosanct.

When I was first ordained, I truly believed that there was a correct way and a wrong way of being church, of doing ministry. Proper liturgy needed to be said around communion and right beliefs were required for baptism. There were things that were proper and things that were not. Over time, though, my rigidity has softened. The first time I was asked to baptize a baby who had died, I did so without hesitation even though I had been taught that it was not necessary and, theologically speaking, incorrect. I baptized the baby out of compassion for the mother who needed to know in a tangible, visceral way that God loved her baby so she could begin the long journey of healing. The first time I was asked to officiate at a commitment service for two men, I did so without worrying about what I had been taught. While I was willing to break these kinds of "rules" to provide what I saw as compassionate pastoral care, it took a lot longer for me to really let go of the idea that the psychological needs of the person should be more carefully considered than should be what I understood to be proper, or right, theology.

Early in my ministry at a state psychiatric hospital, a patient asked me to bless a bottle of shampoo and conditioner. My inclination was to say no. In the United Church of Christ, we do not bless objects and don't very often bless animals or even people. Yet, here was this person, so anxious and fearful, asking me to bless these bottles. It turns out that it actually was a good thing for me to do. This person lived with symptoms of schizophrenia that created the delusion that there were demons who attacked her in the shower. If the shampoo and conditioner were blessed, the demons could not attack. The two of us went into the chapel and I blessed those bottles and I offered the patient a blessing as well. Yet it was me who was most blessed that day.

I spoke the Word of Life in that simple ritual and set myself free. From that day on, what mattered the most to me were the needs of the individual or community rather than all my notions about properly administered sacraments and solid theological practices. I think of the many times Jesus broke the rules to bring healing and hope to a person. If the church did this more often, think of how many more lives would literally be saved.

The Word Living Among Us

When I returned to Princeton Theological Seminary to work toward a Masters of Theology, I took a youth ministry course with Dr. Kenda Creasy Dean.[3] She did two things early in the semester that have stayed with me: First, she gave each of us a diaper pin and told us that we were pregnant with the Holy Spirit and our job was to follow Mary's example of bringing Christ into the world and stepping out of the way. The diaper pin has a spot on my office shelves to this day. Second, she told us that if we call

---

3 At the time I studied with her, Kenda Creasy Dean was writing, with Ron Foster, *The Godbearing Life: The Art of Soul Tending for Youth Ministry* (Nashville: Upper Room, 1998). The class I took with Dr. Dean and, later, my reading of that book, reshaped my understanding of youth ministry and helped me formulate my own theology of youth ministry.

ourselves Christians, then we are the closest thing to Jesus Christ anyone will encounter.

At the time I took the class, I had about ten years of youth ministry experience, some before ordination and some after. Her words changed how I saw youth ministry and how I understood my own story. Before that class with Kenda, I hadn't given much thought to Mary's role in Christianity. It had never occurred to me that Christianity came into being because an unwed, teenage mother said yes to God. Being pregnant out of wedlock was a stoneable offense. She carried and gave birth to the One who changed everything.

It finally registered with me that no one is outside of God's reach. No one is beyond redemption, and everyone can be transformed by the Spirit, even me. I stopped seeing my childhood as something to be overcome, survived, and kept in the deep, dark places of my being. Instead, I began to see my experiences as a significant part of my story, and my story as part of the Christian story. I had this amazing sense that I would one day find a place in Paul's "great cloud of witnesses" (Heb. 12:1). In other words, I discovered that I had a strength and a power that was more than just my own.

If Mary, of all people, could be chosen to bring Christ into the world, then I, despite everything, could be forgiven. I continued to struggle with the sense that I had done unforgivable things. I had tried to kill myself. I had an eating disorder that was more or less under control by the time I was ordained at 25. By 27, I had been married and divorced. Surely, that wasn't forgivable, either. I had assumed responsibility for the abuse of my childhood, also. It is common for children who have been abused to think that it is their fault, and I certainly did. How could God forgive these things?

It's taken me years and two failed marriages to learn some important lessons that have allowed me to live into the forgiveness God freely offers. First, I finally realized that I had done nothing to deserve the childhood I had had. God was also not responsible for the bad things that had happened to me. My family of origin is riddled with untreated alcoholism and mental illness. In spite of what pop theology suggests, everything does not happen according to the will of God, or even for a reason. Bad things happen to innocent people because human beings choose what God would rather we did not. People make these kinds of choices all the time. The results or consequences of these poor choices go on to cause harm, often for generations. While this way of thinking helps me to understand better the choices my parents and others made, explanations are not excuses; people are still responsible for their actions. However, understanding how people come to make the choices they do has helped me to defuse the anger and pain of having been victimized.

Second, I learned that it is impossible to love someone enough for them to love themselves. While God's love has the power to transform lives, my love does not guarantee transformation. In hindsight, my first two marriages were to people who needed saving from themselves. I was unable to heal their brokenness, brokenness that they were unable to acknowledge in themselves. As each marriage ended, I felt hurt, angry, and betrayed even as each person I was married to blamed me for the divorce. It took me years to understand that my love alone was not enough to save them from themselves, their own pain—their psychache. I thought my love for them would be enough. In fact, when I told the officiant at our commitment ceremony that I was sure my (first) wife was an alcoholic, she suggested that my love might be what my wife needed to learn to love herself. The power of those words from someone I respected held me in that relationship for years. Looking back on both marriages, it is clear that I thought that if I gave either of my former spouses what I so desperately wanted, they could love themselves, and then love me the way I needed to be loved. In both cases I was wrong and ended up feeling used and hurt and rejected.

The third thing I learned on the path to forgiving myself is that no one will ever choose me over their addiction. Just as I could not choose anyone over my eating disorder, no one would choose me over their alcohol or drugs. I remember once when John was trying to find something that would motivate me to stop losing weight, if not gain a pound or two, he suggested that maybe we wouldn't talk if I continued to lose weight. That struck such fear in me that I can feel it to this day. As much as I might have wanted to, I couldn't have chosen him. Fortunately, that plan was abandoned fairly quickly. Unfortunately, I didn't apply that lesson of powerlessness over addiction to my relationships until many years later, after I had finally realized that there wasn't so much for which to forgive myself.

In the years since then, as a clinician and pastor I've accompanied many people in the struggle to find self-forgiveness and make room for divine forgiveness. The problem always seems to lie with the individual feeling responsible for all the awful, traumatic, abusive things they have survived. On top of that, many who were Christian believed that they were outside of Christ's love for the world.

In my years as a clinical chaplain at a state psychiatric hospital, I spent hours in conversation with people who fully believed that Christ is "Lord and Savior" of everyone—except them. We would talk about their histories, how they got to the hospital, what diagnosis they were given, and who they thought God was. Always, they would tell me that God is love and that through Christ we all have an opportunity to experience that amazing love. All except them. They had the sense that the abuse they'd lived through or the illness they struggled with was proof that God did not love them. Consequently, they were unforgivable. The conversation would go something like this:

> **Me:** What have you done that is so unforgivable?
> **Patient:** Nothing, really.
> **Me:** So God loves the whole world but not you?
> **Patient:** Well, that doesn't make sense.
> **Me:** No. No, it doesn't. Do you think it could be possible that God loves you as much as God loves everyone else?
> **Patient:** Maybe... Are you sure God loves me even though I have this diagnosis and bad things have happened?
> **Me:** Yes. Yes, I am very sure.

Forgiveness, forgiving ourselves or accepting God's forgiveness, is a mile marker on the journey toward wholeness. One of the reasons that suicide can have appeal for those who have survived trauma or those who live with symptoms of serious mental illness is that such persons interpret those experiences as God's judgment. If you already believe that God is punishing you through trauma or illness and there seems to be no way to please this God, then the risk of eternal damnation isn't all that significant. Gently helping a person to release God from the constricting bonds of this kind of belief system will increase the likelihood of healing. If suffering is not inflicted on us as a punishment from God, then it becomes possible to conceive of a God who is present through our suffering. It becomes possible to believe that God's love has been constant, and will continue to be so.

Expanding a person's understanding of God from a personal, judgmental, punishing God to a God who wants only goodness, hope, and wholeness for God's people is difficult work. I don't know that I ever really thought God was actively punishing me so much as I had assumed that I was not worth God's attention and care. This wasn't any more helpful theologically than the belief that God punishes us through traumatic events or illnesses. Both perspectives leave a person alone and suffering and assuming responsibility for the pain, which can result in an overwhelming sense of guilt and shame. Just telling me that I was wrong about God wasn't helpful or healing. I don't imagine criticism of this kind would be helpful for anyone else. Embodying Christ and sharing a part of someone's journey toward wholeness? Now that can change everything!

When I encounter someone who struggles with thoughts of suicide or engages in suicidal behavior, in the mix of contributing factors they almost always understand God in a way that is far too small. Note that the people to whom Jesus offers forgiveness in the stories we read don't have to do anything to earn it. Take, for example, the infamous woman who was caught in adultery (Jn. 8:1–11): Jesus didn't judge her. He didn't ask her to explain herself or beg him for forgiveness. Instead, he enabled her to see that everyone sinned in one way or another and she wasn't so different from everyone else. He didn't condemn her or punish her in any way. He simply told her to stop doing what she had been doing.

Using this story, or another like it, to illustrate that Jesus is more likely to offer forgiveness and compassion than judgment and punishment might be what someone needs to change their understanding of who God is. Of course, this theological shift is often gradual and, on its own, cannot eradicate suicidality. However, if it is possible to plant a small seed of hope that God values even sinners (which includes all of us!) enough to offer forgiveness, it becomes more likely that the one trapped in suicidal thinking will take a step toward life.

My experience is that we tend to underestimate just how much people need to know that they are indeed forgivable. One of the greatest gifts Christianity has to offer is God's unconditional love. "If we confess our sins, he who is faithful and just will forgive us our sins and cleanse us from all unrighteousness" (1 Jn. 1:9). Guilt and shame have the power to destroy a person; they feed the psychache. This is especially true when one has assumed responsibility for events out of one's control, as is often the case with survivors of childhood abuse. The healing power of confessing sins and hearing words of the assurance of pardon is astonishing. Even when a person falsely assumes an overwhelming sense of guilt and shame, the ability to name that guilt and shame and hear words of forgiveness has meaning.

Over the years, I have encountered congregations that have stopped including a prayer of confession in their weekly liturgy. They do this because the idea of sin makes them uncomfortable. They somehow think that if they acknowledge their sin, the ways in which they break relationship with themselves, their neighbors, creation, or God, they admit to being worthless. This connection between sin and worthlessness is an erroneous one. If we believe the statement in John 3:16 about just how much God loves the whole of creation, then the human capacity for sin does not remove any of our value. Would you give your life, or the life of your child, for something that is worthless? Absolutely not. Why would God?

Removing prayers of confession from public worship removes a potential protective factor for those struggling with suicidality. If there is no reminder that God loves us more than we can imagine and that God forgives us when (if not before) we ask, then why would we ask? A reminder of just how much God values each of us is one of the most necessary elements in a worship service. Who knows how many lives have been saved with words such as: "God is merciful and just and forgives all our sins and sets us free to be the whole people of God"?

What Your Congregation Can Do Now:

- Emphasize God's unconditional love for all persons no matter what, without exceptions. (See also Appendix F: Scripture Verses and Stories that Emphasize Hope.)

- Accompany people in their suffering without trying to fix them.

- Be present. Show up even when it is uncomfortable.

- Recognize the importance of prayers of confession and words of assurance of pardon and use them. (See also Appendix G: Prayers.)

- Be profligate with your blessings for individuals and the gathered community.

Chapter 3

The Body of Christ Is Fearful

*"The thief comes only to steal and kill and destroy. I came that
they may have life, and have it abundantly."*
—John 10:10

After college and before seminary, I took a year off and
embarked on a series of jobs. First, I spent the summer working at
a Girl Scout camp in Western Massachusetts. Then I returned to
Allentown, Pennsylvania, where I had been in college and rented
an apartment with one of my senior year roommates. For the first
weeks, I worked for the college in the same office in which I had
done some of my work study. After about six weeks, I was hired as
a social worker in a court-mandated afterschool care program. In
addition, I was the youth coordinator for a church in Bethlehem,
Pennsylvania.

On the surface, everything looked great. I was a normal,
healthy weight; I was in a relationship with a boy I loved; and
it appeared that the troubles of my past were over. This wasn't
exactly true. While I went to work diligently and excelled as a
social worker, I did not yet grasp how much this kind of work
touched my own barely contained pain. Throughout that year
as I engaged with kids from the projects who were identified as
"emotionally disturbed," and with hurting kids from the church,

I kept silent about my own pain. I was afraid of what it would mean if I admitted how lost I still felt.

As a result of my need to keep silent about my on-going struggles, at least once a month I binged and purged. I skipped meals whenever I could do so without drawing attention, and I frequently thought about dying. The problem was that I couldn't tell anyone. The therapist I had been seeing in college thought I was well enough to "graduate" from therapy. Although John was still in my life since the church he served was less than hour from Muhlenberg (where I had gone to college), he had no idea what I struggled with. And I could not tell him.

I didn't tell anyone for more than a year. During my first semester at Princeton Theological Seminary, I had a class with Dr. Christie Neuger.[1] The last class of the semester was on counseling women in crisis. As she talked, I was flooded with memories from my childhood, things I had long repressed and denied had ever happened. During that lecture, I was inundated with images from childhood. It was like watching a movie of the worst moments of my life, and I felt completely powerless. With these newly recalled memories of physical, sexual, and emotional abuse, my suicidal thoughts increased from very occasional to practically daily. My constant fantasy was that I would go to sleep and not wake up, or that I'd contract a fatal illness that had no cure. With these revelations and an increase in suicidality, I returned to my mother's house for Christmas break. There I was met with more memories and an increase in the frequency of some deeply disturbing nightmares.

Returning to school from Christmas break, I knew I had to do *something* because I wasn't sleeping or eating, and couldn't focus on anything, including impending final exams. After a study group, I ended up talking to Doug, the TA for Christie's class. I told him about the flood of memories. He listened carefully and validated my feelings before recommending that I talk with Christie, who could help me find a therapist who could help me navigate these newly surfacing memories. He held space that day,

---

1 The class I took with Christie Cozad Neuger was Introduction to Pastoral Care and Counseling. Dr. Neuger would later publish *Counseling Women* (Minneapolis: Fortress, 2001). This book remains on my shelf and is an excellent resource.

listening without judgment and without trying to excuse or fix what had happened, as I struggled to say what had happened to me. Most importantly, he sat and listened and did not confirm my fears that I was a horrible person who did not belong in seminary. At the time, I didn't even notice the silence that lay shattered around me. I spoke some of my pain out loud and nothing bad happened. In fact, it was only good.

When I met with Christie, she also listened and validated my feelings. In addition, she mirrored an incredible amount of pain. I remember not understanding the pain I saw on her face. In thinking about it later, her response made me think for the first time that the pain I endured and the pain I still carried was real. This was the focus of therapy for me for the remainder of my seminary years. I had to find a way to say these things out loud and stop running from them.

The therapist to whom Christie referred me was a good match for me. She was a pastoral psychotherapist and affirmed my call to ministry while creating space for me to work toward healing the brokenness. Consequently, my seminary years changed many things for me. I did finally put an end to my eating disorder behavior. I enjoyed a sense of community and developed some lasting friendships. While I shared some of my experiences in papers I wrote for unsuspecting professors and teaching assistants, they, along with pastors and friends, advised me not to share these experiences with others if I wanted to be ordained. That advice came without the givers knowing that I still had some very weird thoughts about food, my body, and exercise, and that I often had suicidal fantasies. Fortunately, sometimes I was able to break the silence and speak my truth to my therapist. Too often, though, shame kept the words tightly inside me.

"For [Jesus] came to seek out and to save the lost." (Lk. 19:10)

Well into my seminary years, I still suffered from psychache. I knew that I wouldn't kill myself because I was sure that God would not continue to love me if I chose suicide. For many reasons, I never gave voice to this fear. It would mean both admitting that I wasn't sure of God's love for me *and* acknowledging that I still had suicidal thoughts. The upside of keeping this secret was that no one tried to address the theology behind my thinking. No one assured me that I would "go to hell" if I died by suicide, which was good. In addition, no one rushed in to remove my fear that if I died by suicide God would never love me. This fear, for me, was a protective factor against engaging in further suicidal behavior. It was good that no one rushed in to assure me of God's eternal and steadfast love for me because without the fear of losing God's love, I would most certainly have engaged in suicidal behavior and, likely, died. (See Appendix B: Resources for Clergy, particularly the first section, "The Moral and Ethical Responsibility.") My theology around suicide was something I was left to ponder for myself.

However, as I began to talk with my therapist about the abuse of my childhood, I thought of suicide less frequently. I was able to shift the "blame" for what had happened onto my parents who permitted my brother to continue to torment me when they could have intervened and could have worked harder to create a loving, validating family. I remember that my mother once admitted that she knew he "was mean to me" when we were left alone, but that she and my father didn't want to do anything that would "make it worse." Their misplaced sense of powerlessness nearly cost me my life and it contributed significantly to the psychache growing in me. During seminary, I figured out that a deep sense of shame and worthlessness kept that pain alive.

This secret underneath my secrets came out in an unexpected way. At a typical youth group meeting in my field education church during my last year in seminary, the associate pastor, Tim, and I were leading a discussion on peer pressure. It was all the stuff one might expect in the early '90s—kids were struggling with alcohol, drugs, sex, grades, sports, etc. One of the girls finally burst out with, "You don't know! You don't know how much pressure there is to be perfect!" She went on tearfully to list her struggles with her grades and sports and her parents' expectations of her. Tim looked at me as if to say, "This one's yours," and I told them the story of my own adolescence. I didn't go into detail, but I included my overdose and my eating disorder. The tone of the meeting shifted and become much more real after that.

When the meeting was over, Tim and I debriefed. He was telling me how great the meeting was. I lost it. I confessed, through uncontrollable tears, that I didn't think God loved me. Where was Christ during the traumatic times in my life? Where was Christ when I wanted to die? Where was Christ when I fought so hard for recovery? Where was Christ if he loved me so much? Tim kept quiet and let me come to the realization on my own. Christ was present in those bleakest moments. Christ surrounded me with a faithful community and people who embodied God's unconditional love. Christ's own heart broke when the pain was more than I could bear. Christ remained present, waiting for me to see, feel, and accept the love, forgiveness, and healing Christ offers everyone, even me.

In 1 Corinthians 12, Paul reminds us that the church is one body made up of many members. The beauty of this is that the stronger members are charged with caring for the weaker, more vulnerable members. In my mind this passage is intricately connected to the story of Jesus saving the woman caught in adultery (Jn. 8:1–11). Jesus challenged those with power to throw stones only if they had no sin themselves. Individually, we all sin, we all hurt, we all fall short. However, when we come together, Christ commands us to care for those among us who are the most vulnerable.

This is what John and the members of that church in Hyannis did for me. This is what Tim did for me that night after the youth group meeting. They cared for me when I was at my most vulnerable. Like Christ with the nameless woman, there was no condemnation, no judgment—only love and an invitation to live in freedom from the sins I held against myself. This is church at its best. When church can set aside issues of budget, building, and butts in the pews—all its fears—to care for those who are most vulnerable, then church is what it was meant to be, namely, *lifesaving*.

Healing from Within

That long-ago night in a basement youth room with Tim as mentor, pastor, and friend was a pivotal and transformative moment for me. However, emotional and spiritual healing happen gradually. By no measure has my journey been pain-free since then. That night, though, I spoke my deepest, most pain-filled secret that kept me tied to the void and nourished the psychache. I spoke it out loud and it turned out to be anything but true. Deeper healing could finally begin.

These days, I am not afraid of much (large snakes, spiders, and sharks aside) and I don't waste time worrying about anything. Yes, I get stressed and anxious in certain situations and I'm sometimes slow to realize when my feelings need more of my attention. However, my days of fear and worry are behind me. I lived through abuse, years of suicidality, an eating disorder, broken relationships, two failed marriages, rejection by the church (this experience will be discussed in a later chapter), unemployment, and near homelessness. What could I possibly have to be afraid of after all of that?

Once I could name my fear that God did not love me and thereby discover that God had in fact always loved me, I found a degree of freedom. It took a long time before it changed the way I viewed myself in the world, but I was free enough to finish seminary, receive a call to a church, and be ordained.

I was the first person in my seminary class to receive a call. The search committee of that church made a point of telling me that they had interviewed 26 candidates for the associate pastor position before they got to me. At that moment, I was certain they were not going to pick me. I was 24 years old with only a few years of part-time student ministry under my belt, and that mostly with youth. Surely, one of those other candidates was better qualified. Well, that committee didn't think so, and I was called to be the associate pastor of a large, vibrant church in Massachusetts.

Due to scheduling conflicts, my ordination service was six months after I started my ministry. I remember confessing to Tim that I thought the church had made a mistake in calling me, that I had no real idea what I was doing, and that most of the time I felt I was making it up. I felt as if I was fooling the congregation and waiting for them to find out that I was clueless. Almost as if to prove the point, when I was giving Tim a tour of the church, we got lost in the building and I had trouble finding my way back to my office. As usual, Tim was wise. He pointed out that the search committee chose me for good reasons, that the only one I was fooling was me, and that I could do the work of ministry just fine.

By grace, after that I managed to separate my personal doubts from my professional ones. During those first few years of ordained ministry, I fully embraced my call to ministry and discovered some of the gifts I had been given. It was a good thing, too. Looking back, I'm amazed by the number of people who came to me confessing their own secrets. Drug use. Alcohol addiction. Pornography. Sex. All the things that people do to try to fill the void and ease the pain, they confessed to me, seeking the hope, absolution, and new life the church is well-equipped to give.

I was startled by the people who came to me to speak of emptiness. More than one middle-aged person has come into my various offices over the years to say things like, "I have everything I ever thought I wanted. So why do I feel so empty?" These are pillars of the church, leaders in the community, highly paid professional women and men. They tell me their stories and I hold their pain and offer hope in exchange. My inevitable response to their confession of emptiness is to ask where God is in their lives. And most of them don't really know.

They tell me of a distant, impersonal, judgmental God, a God far too small for the grown-up lives they are living. They speak of a God who demands perfection in exchange for favors. Or they don't actually think of God as personal at all. They think of church as a place to come for community, for kinship, for connecting with people, but they aren't sure what they believe about God. That's hard to hear, sometimes. It's harder still not just to blurt out that Christ can fill the void better than all the money, sex, drugs, or whatever else they've tried. But I can't speak those words too soon. I have to wait through the silence, through the tears, to the moment when they can no longer deny that Christ is present, loves them, and does not require any degree of perfection. Sometimes, the most vulnerable among us are the ones who seem the strongest.

When our faith communities perpetuate the myth of perfection, we are inadvertently contributing to people's pain. In those congregations in which "proper" clothes and "proper" behavior are still required, where does that leave those who might not have the means to buy nice clothes, or those who lack the capacity to control some of their behaviors? When we focus on perfection being a means of displaying the power of one's faith, what are we saying to those who most keenly feel their imperfections? Where in the Bible does it tell us that to be a good Christian is to be perfect? If you are thinking of Matthew 5:48, in which Jesus states, "Be perfect, therefore, as your heavenly Father is perfect," this verse has nothing to do with the perfection of performance or appearance. Here, Jesus is inviting us to endeavor to live into and to embody the abundant love God offers. Jesus is asking us to enter into a process of loving perfectly, a process that will take a lifetime, a loving community, and the power of the Holy Spirit to pursue.

When we take out of context this invitation to be perfect and try to live according to social expectations, we significantly limit our capacity to love, to create faith-filled community, and to embody Christ. For those who live with depression, suicidality, and other forms of mental illness, perfection of appearance or performance or compliance with social norms is often not possible. If Christ only loves us when we are perfectly behaved or perfectly groomed, or socially successful, then we are already lost. If a church requires a certain kind of life or appearance, then people can become very good at hiding the imperfections. The problem then becomes that they are not truly connected to the community. If the community accepts the presented image, then the person can conclude that they wouldn't be accepted as readily, if at all, if people really knew what's hidden away in the secret corners of themselves.

Human beings need to be in relationship; it is not good for any of us to be alone (Gen. 2:18). Perhaps even more than relationships with individuals, we need to be in community. Without a sense of belonging somewhere, the human spirit withers, the void threatens to consume us, and the seeds of psychache begin to grow. If we are paying attention, church can be that place of belonging for anyone, *if* we don't let our rules and traditions prevent us from creating a safe space for all vulnerable people, members and seekers alike, who come to us seeking to be saved from their own isolation.

In most of the miracle stories in the gospels, we focus on the healing of the individual. We are distracted by the fact that the formerly blind see again, those unable to walk can walk again, lepers are cleansed, and the dead live again, and we miss the truly miraculous events: that Jesus re-membered those who were ritually unclean outcasts. He saw them and literally and metaphorically *re-membered* them: he rejoined them to their communities. If we want church to be lifesaving, then this is our task: to see those who are on the margins of existence—physically, emotionally, socially, or spiritually—and offer them a place of healing where they can be re-membered, rejoined to the Body of Christ. Prolonged isolation in body, mind, or spirit leads to death. Belonging to a community that truly welcomes everyone as they are and embodies Christ's love without condition is the necessary antidote to deadly isolation.

What Your Congregation Can Do Now:

- Learn to be more comfortable with those who struggle to give voice to their pain or painful experiences. Learn to listen without judgement to their experiences. Validate their worth as human beings and make room in the church for those who are clearly less than "perfect."

- Be sure that youth have a safe space in which to share their experiences with adults who have training in listening skills and can keep appropriate boundaries.

- Remember that everyone can experience shame, psychache, and emptiness. The task of any church is to offer a place of welcome, inclusion, and acceptance.

- Practice being a nonjudgmental community grounded in God's steadfast love, open to all who walk through the doors.

- Practice compassionate care that embodies Christ.

Chapter 4

The Body of Christ Is Resilient

May the God of hope fill you with all joy and peace in believing, so that you may abound in hope by the power of the Holy Spirit.

—Romans 15:13

By the time I was 30, I had been a social worker, earned two master's degrees, been divorced, and was serving my second church as an associate pastor. I'd also survived the abuse of my childhood, years of suicidality, an eating disorder, and more than one heartbreak. I was okay...but not really. I was still keeping secret my feelings and struggles with depression.

After receiving my second master's degree from Princeton Theological Seminary, I accepted a call to a large Presbyterian church not far from the seminary campus. I was one of several associate pastors and my job was primarily children's and family ministry. It seemed like a good fit at the time. It wasn't long, though, before I realized that things weren't quite right. I would sleep through most of my days off, sometimes only getting out of bed to visit friends. Even though I was working with a spiritual director at the time, I didn't talk about this growing depression.

What I did talk about was the difficult situation at the church. I was sure the senior pastor was an alcoholic, even though no one else seemed to think so. He was rigid in his expectations and had no problem raising his voice with staff members and parishioners alike, and he often had the smell of alcohol on his breath. At one point a parishioner came to me with the concern that the senior pastor had a brain tumor because his behavior was erratic and he sometimes slurred his words. That was a difficult conversation to have and one that I probably didn't handle as wisely as I should have done. It was many months before the truth of the situation at that church came out. In the meantime, I felt as if I were drowning. During those months, I struggled with eating-disorder thoughts (believing I was fat, counting calories, constantly thinking about how to lose weight) and an increase in suicidality. I wished on a daily basis that I would go to sleep and not wake up. Sometimes I would think about the medications I could take so I could, in fact, go to sleep and not wake up. I felt helpless, powerless, and stuck.

Then one day I saw an advertisement for a youth chaplain for the town of Harwich, Massachusetts. While I wasn't thrilled about the idea of moving to within 13 miles of where I had grown up, I was enthralled by the idea of this position. The youth chaplain would be responsible for meeting the needs of youth who were outside the existing church and secular structures, and would work with seven churches, the school district, and the police department to meet these needs. I remember calling Tim and telling him that I thought this was the perfect job for me.

And indeed, after about a year at the Presbyterian church, I moved back to Cape Cod to be the first youth chaplain for the town of Harwich. It was exciting and amazing, and all traces of depression were gone—for the moment. I was pretty busy during my first few months, more than I would have anticipated.

A teen died by suicide when I'd only been in town for a couple of months. She was not a member of any of the churches, and the only other place large enough to have her memorial service was the high school auditorium. Looking back, besides the location (see Appendix B: Resources for Clergy, "Funeral Dos and Don'ts"), I made many other mistakes with that service in my rush to assure family members and friends that the one who had died by suicide was at peace. This wasn't my first memorial service for someone who had suicided and I did what I had done previously: I assured family members and friends that the pain had ended and their loved one was at peace. Fortunately, the subsequent suicides and suicidal behaviors of others in town did not involve people who were among those grieving that day.

Many progressive clergy make this mistake of rushing to offer comfort and hope to the survivors of suicide loss. In its own way, it can be just as dangerous as rushing to affirm that the one who died by suicide is condemned to hell. Depending on the audience, either of these positions can lead to contagion: *more* people engaging in suicidal behavior or dying by suicide. In a public setting, it is best to assume that there is at least one person in the room who is actively struggling with suicidal thoughts and plans. If that person hears that God welcomes the one who died by suicide and that they are free from pain and at peace, then they have received a message that could tacitly give them permission to suicide. Similarly, those who have survived suicide loss and hear a message that their loved one is in hell could decide to suicide as well, so that their loved one will not be alone in hell for all eternity. (See Appendix E: Resources for Suicide Loss Survivors.) Speaking publicly at a memorial service for one who has died by suicide is a delicate balancing act. Clergy have a moral and ethical responsibility to navigate the waters of safe messaging while offering authentic words of faith and hope. (See Appendix B: Resources for Clergy, "Moral and Ethical Responsibility" for when responding to suicidality or suicide or suicide loss survivors, and "Funeral Dos and Don'ts": using safe messaging practices.)

Back in those days, I just wanted to alleviate the pain that survivors were feeling. I was also struggling with a strange sense that any suicides and suicidal behavior that I encountered in Harwich were somehow personal. I was desperate to find a way to give hope to these teens who killed themselves, and others who wanted to die. Yes, I showed up. Yes, I listened. Yes, I saw them and their own struggles with the overwhelming, unbearable pain of their psychache. Yet I felt helpless when a teacher died by suicide a few months later, and more helpless still each time I was called to the emergency room for a teen who had endeavored to kill him- or herself.

This pushed me to examine the shame I still carried from my experiences with suicidality. I worked with a spiritual director and I spent a lot of time thinking, reading, and writing, desperate to discern how I could communicate the hope I had found in Christ. What I discovered about myself in the process was completely unexpected.

One afternoon, I went to the movies to give myself a break. I saw *In & Out*, a movie in which a teacher, who has not yet realized he is gay, is outed by one of his students. Driving back to my apartment, I remember thinking, "That could be me." I dismissed this idea, believing that it was only loneliness leading me to think this way. It wasn't loneliness, though. Strangely, it was an answer to prayer. I kept asking God to guide me to someone whom I could love and who could love me. I was tired of relationships that ended in pain, anger, and frustration. I was tired of working so hard to get someone to love me. In later years, I learned to be a little more specific with my prayers.

In December of 1998, I went to a friend's Christmas party. When the party was over, I stayed to help clean up. My friend was telling me about a New Year's Eve party she and her partner were planning. She said that they would have invited me, but it was for lesbians only. I laughed and said, "Well, if I could get a date..." I thought I was joking. As it turns out, I was not. Not at all. From the moment the words left my mouth, I knew they were true. I am gay. I was so distracted by this revelation that I got lost going home. It should have taken me an hour at most, and it took me three. I did end up going to that New Year's Eve party, though without a date.

Things moved pretty quickly in my life after that. I met a woman and began dating her. I started to tell my friends that I was gay. Then there was the challenge of what to do about work. The few friends and colleagues I had told advised me not to tell the Youth Ministries. Hating the idea of keeping secrets, knowing how destructive secrets can be, I chose to tell the Ecumenical Youth Ministries Board of Directors. I wanted them to know, so that if questions were asked they would be supportive. I was, after all, ordained in the United Church of Christ, where being gay shouldn't be a problem, right? I was UCC, and two of the churches involved in the ministry were UCC; the rest were not.

My trust in the church was misplaced that day.

Essentially, I ended up resigning because the Board of Directors wanted me to come out to the governing bodies of all seven churches that made up the ministry, the school superintendent, and the chief of police. This seemed absurd to me. Who were they to tell me to whom I had to come out? As an alternative, they suggested that I quietly resign for "personal reasons." That wasn't going to happen either. I told my story to a reporter and it became front page news. It was a decade before I was accepted for a permanent, fulltime ministry position again.

Claiming a Place at the Table

Imagine the Christian story without Mary of Magdala. Jesus healed her of her seven demons (Lk. 8:2) and she became a faithful disciple. She later bore witness to the crucifixion, and the Resurrection. What if she had not? What if Jesus' existing disciples had not allowed the newly freed Mary Magdalene to join them and she had faded back into the crowd? How much richness would have been lost? Who would have borne witness to Jesus' death? To whom would he have appeared on that first Easter morning? Who would have been such a faithful, loving witness to Christ's presence and power?

When I came out to myself, I had such a profound sense of wholeness. This sexual identity piece had been what I was missing. I saw my claiming of my full self as something that could only strengthen my capacity for ministry with the youth of Harwich, and for ministry in general. But that is not the welcome I received. People were afraid, afraid that I could somehow make their kids gay. Someone on the Board of Directors had the audacity to ask me what I would say if some of the kids I met with regularly also came out, as if my being gay were contagious. My response was to point out that, statistically, I could be certain that LGBTQ youth were already present, that they had a higher risk for suicide and suicidality, and that the high rate of suicidal behavior for the youth in town was likely related, at least in part, to issues of sexual identity. In 1998, there were gay kids in Harwich even if the board members weren't ready to admit it.

When I left that ministry, I was more heartbroken than I had ever been before. Church had been the safe place of my childhood. After ordination, church wasn't the same kind of safe place, yet it had remained a place where I was validated, valued, and affirmed. Now it wasn't. While I was preaching and teaching about the youth ministry in Harwich, several churches had approached me asking if I wanted to apply to be their pastor. Suddenly, none of them wanted anything to do with me. The only thing that had changed was that I was now a woman in a relationship with a woman.

Though I felt whole in ways I hadn't been before, being rejected by the church that had loved and protected me was devastating. I belonged to the United Church of Christ, a denomination that had been the first to ordain gay and lesbian people—more than 20 years before. Yet, I was no longer good enough to serve as anyone's pastor. This rejection made me question my worth as much as my harmful childhood had. While I did not engage in eating-disorder behavior at this time, I had a steady stream of thoughts about being fat, needing to lose weight, counting calories, and exercising more. Some days it was exhausting to battle this constant stream of negativity going around and around in my head. Other days, I wished I could go to sleep and not wake up. I was exhausted and overwhelmed with a sense that I was no longer "good enough" even for the church that had been such a lifesaving factor in my life.

About a year later, I was offered the opportunity to be the interim pastor at a small church in Weymouth, Massachusetts. I had been available to provide pastoral care at a time when crisis hit the congregation while their interim had been having his own health issues. When it became clear that their interim was unable to continue, they decided to offer me the position. Half the people remaining at that church left when I came in because they did not want a gay pastor; they did not want to become a "gay church." While it was somewhat healing to have my call to ministry once again affirmed, the homophobia that lurked in the hidden spaces of that congregation made it challenging to be there.

For two and a half years, I served that congregation, and they grew. When a group of folks began to advocate for me to become the settled pastor, things became more tense. The homophobia that had been hidden became much more blatant. More than anything else, this congregation feared becoming a gay church. Leaving them pained me much more than had leaving Harwich.

I struggled to figure out how congregations could be so hateful and hurtful, when Jesus never was. Think of all the people Jesus re-membered—the lepers, the blind, the woman caught in adultery, the Samaritan woman, the Gerasene demoniac, and all the other unwanted, unclean, "othered" people. They managed to move from the margins toward the center of community because Jesus saw them and made them whole. Jesus focused so much of his ministry on re-membering people. *How is it that the church has become so proficient at dis-membering people?* Jesus made a point of restoring people who lived on the margins and beyond to the fullness of life and community. Too many of today's churches at worst pass judgment on those folks and at best ignore them.

In the days after I left that interim position, I felt dis-membered once again. It made no sense to me that the church felt justified in rejecting me because I was not the person they thought I was supposed to be. In doing so, the deepest fears of my childhood—that I was not good enough for God to love me—appeared once again confirmed. If God sent Jesus to show us the way of love and remind us that hatred, violence, and destruction do not have the final say, how can any church, any Body of Christ, practice judgment and rejection that cuts *any* human being off from community? Surely, this is not what God desires for us.

Self-Worth Is More than Pop Psychology

It had taken me years to figure out that I had value as a human being, that I was truly a beloved child of God. And while that discovery was still fresh and fragile, the church had rejected me. To survive, I had to separate God from the church, which was a tricky thing to do. I'd finally gotten to the place in my life at which I thought God loved me more often than I thought God did not, only to be totally rejected by the church. It was confusing and painful, and made me question my value as a person over the next few years.

Once again, my salvation came through the Holy Spirit. While I continued in an unhealthy personal relationship that had pulled me away from most of my friends, I was hired as a pastoral psychotherapist. I told the director of the center that I had not had any clinical experience, though I had had enough education, and she was unconcerned. Looking back, I don't know why she wasn't more concerned, except that working as a therapist turned out to be redemptive in many ways.

Most of my clients at the counseling center were women and girls with depression, eating disorders, or other self-harming behaviors. Even though they were reluctant at first, many developed a trust in me. They would confess their secrets, and we'd work toward healthier responses to pain and sadness. It turned out that the worst experiences of my life were very helpful because, if nothing else, I knew the pain was survivable. Knowing this allowed me to hold space with and offer genuine hope for these girls, women, men, and families that came to me for help. Once again, I was learning to trust my gifts for ministry—not the ministry I had ever thought I would be doing, but ministry nonetheless.

While I was doing this good work, the Spirit had something else in mind as well. A small group of people came to me from the church where I had been an interim a few years before. They had been asked to leave that church for various reasons, and they wanted a church where no one would ever be asked to leave. After many conversations and a lot of prayer, I agreed to be the gathering pastor of this new church. A new church start was not the sort of ministry to which I ever thought I'd be called. Yet, there I was, and Promise Church was born.

During these years, I started to feel good about myself as a therapist and as a pastor. I had gifts and skills, and God was using me for good purpose. It was just that my personal life was a mess. My marriage came to an unhappy end, and I felt like a failure yet again. What kind of pastor could I be, what kind of therapist could I be, if I was divorced for a *second* time? For the next 18 months, I struggled with as deep a depression as I had ever had.

This time, at least, I knew what was behind it: I was afraid that I was unlovable; and, if I wasn't lovable, then what good was I? Sure, people liked me. I had friends. But the relationships that *really* mattered to me were: the one I had with my mother, the one I had with the church, and the romantic ones. I lived in fear of becoming like my mother. She had a series of relationships, all with married men, and she was never happy. She wasn't thrilled with my coming out, but she hadn't been particularly supportive prior to that, either. Whenever my life was in transition, my mother would ask me if I was going to "get a real job." For her, ministry of any kind—in the parish or in the community—didn't count as "real." In her view, I was wasting my life; I should have been a doctor or a veterinarian or, at the very least, a teacher so I could have summers "off." For her, real work meant a paycheck that more than paid all the bills. Whenever I tried to talk to her, my mother had a way of making me feel worthless.

In the past, I could count on church to be a safe place. While Promise Church is a dedicated, wonderful group of people, it wasn't a place of safety or affirmation for me. During my years with them, the Conference refused to see them as a valid new church start. I was told over and over again that "there was no money," or that the vision of inclusion the church had "was not sustainable," or that "they didn't have enough members" to be a real church. Lots of excuses, and no support. It was hard not to take it personally *especially* when, after I left that church, they were suddenly granted official new church status.

My relationship with my mother and my relationship with the church were full of frustration and rejection in those days. Throw in leaving the nine-year relationship that had evolved into my second marriage, and it was hard for me to feel good about who I was. I was a good pastor. I was a good therapist. But was I worth anything if a person did not need me to fulfill a specific role? Some days, it was really hard to get out of bed and get moving. My fantasies in those days fluctuated between going to sleep and never waking up and being rescued by someone who could fix everything. Fortunately, neither of these things happened.

I had been working with a great therapist for a few years before I left my marriage. Merle Jordan kept me on track. I had learned over the years how to talk about my feelings. I was able to express to Merle how much pain I was in and how much of a failure I felt like. He challenged my thinking and assured me that God was with me. He basically told me that God hadn't gotten me through all the crap just to drop me back in it and leave me there. I didn't exactly believe him, but since these were words I could have said to a number of my own clients, I accepted them and began to pray differently. I wanted to value myself as much as Merle did. I wanted to be in relationship with someone who valued me for myself and not for what I could do for them. Mostly, I wanted to believe that I was worth the effort.

On the Tuesday of Holy Week that year, I was alone in my room praying when I had a vision. At first, I was reluctant to admit that I had had a vision because I thought I had a deal with God. I had had a few experiences in which I had spiritual dreams and I was okay with God communicating with me through dreams. I could tell myself they were just dreams. But a *vision!?* Visions are something else, and I was skeptical about their existence until I had one of my own.

The vision I had was one of intentional community. I saw a place that was a small farm with crops and animals. It had a central building that held a simple sanctuary, office space, and meeting rooms. There was another building that was part working barn and part dormitory. There were two other buildings on the property that were small houses built in a log cabin style. In addition to the fields that were farmed, there was a large wooded area with a beautiful outdoor chapel in the center. People lived and worked here, and the community was self-sustaining. Others came in for retreats. The sense of peace and safety was overwhelming.

I had no idea what that vision meant. Was I supposed to go join a community? Create one? Right then? Or later? I had no clue. When I talked to Tim about it, he suggested that it was a promise for a season of abundance that was going to come into my life. Merle also saw it as a promise, a promise of community that would love and value me. He suggested that perhaps it was an indication that I should begin to value myself as much as God did; not just anyone receives sacred visions.

I knew from professional and personal experience that people who do not see themselves as valuable are more likely to put themselves in risky situations. The youth who sat in my office and told me of participating in parties with drugs, alcohol, and sex because they wanted to be accepted and liked were a reminder of all the self-destructive things I had done. The women and men who sat in the same seats and told me about their marriages to alcoholics and sex addicts and gambling addicts after growing up with parents who engaged in the same kind of behaviors also felt familiar. My story. Their stories. I knew I had to resolve the question of my own value or I would end up repeating the mistakes of my past. Merle often told me, "We gravitate toward what is familiar." My amendment to this statement is: "...until they are done with us or until we are done with them." I was ready to be done with addictions and this pervasive suspicion of worthlessness. I was ready to explore the possibilities of the far less familiar. It was time for me to pull up psychache by its roots and to face into the void. As much as I'd pretended to myself that I'd faced the pain of my childhood and accepted God's love for me, I had to confront this sense of worthlessness before all the work I had done was undone.

What Your Congregation Can Do Now:

- Create a safe space for people to share their stories without judgment.

- Recognize the value of belonging in a loving, accepting community and endeavor to be that community.

- Communicate the gospel in a way that affirms the value of each person as God's beloved.

Chapter 5

The Body of Christ Is Beloved

"God so loved the world that he gave his only Son,
so that everyone who believes in him may not perish but may
have eternal life."

—John 3:16

Over the years, I have heard many therapists describe recovery as peeling away the layers of an onion. This metaphor made me reluctant to engage, because it symbolized my deepest fear, for when you peel away all the layers of an onion, you are left with nothing. If I peeled away all the layers of pain, would I find nothing? If I were not broken beyond repair or worthless beyond redemption, who was I? Would anyone really see me if I were free of pain? This fear may not make sense to anyone who hasn't suffered from psychache, but it was real, and it complicated my journey toward wholeness considerably.

I used to be so afraid of anyone finding out that I had tried to kill myself. I didn't want anyone to think I was crazy. I didn't want to be dismissed. It never occurred to me that my walking around at 102 pounds made me look pretty crazy to most people. While I had promised John and my therapist that I would not try suicide again, I made no such promise about courting death. This is how I described my eating disorder:

"Only a Stray Fantasy"[1]

A little spark goes bang
And a new world grows.
Quickly, too quickly, it encompasses.
No more real life,
No more pain,
Only dreams of what could be,
What may be, someday,
Things that will never be.
The spark grows to an intriguing flame.
Nothing can leave it,
It becomes reality.
All things are perfected.
No faults,
No flaws,
Only perfection.
The flame becomes too hot.
It burns.
It is real,
The one and only reality.
Scorching flames break up innocence.
No more love,
No more happiness,
Only the burning pain,
The pain of losing a fantasy,
Letting it become too real.
No more smiles,
No more cries,
No more laughs,
No more me,
Only a stray fantasy.

For years, I felt lost and alone. The times when I thought most about suicide were the times I felt unloved and unlovable. As an adolescent, I didn't think anyone loved me. My mother had a limited capacity for emotions of any kind, and she was seldom

---

1 I wrote this in the spring of 1983, shortly before I was hospitalized.

demonstrative. In her later years, my mother would always say, "Love you," as we ended any phone conversation. I suppose she did love me, sort of. My mother loved the version of me she constructed for herself. She never understood her sensitive, artist, poet daughter who believed wholeheartedly in God. When I went to seminary, she told people I went to Princeton (that was brag-worthy!), but she would say I was in human services. She always told me that I was wasting my life with poetry and theology. She was quite taken aback each time one of my three books of theological poetry was published. She read two of them, but still could not see me.

That was the real problem for me. Since my own mother could not "see" me, I was skeptical of anyone who thought they did. When people were nice to me, I thought they wanted something or thought I was crazy and needed sympathy. Even now, when I deal with painful emotions, I can contain myself—until someone reaches out in compassion, and then I cry. I am always startled when someone notices that I am in pain. When I sought recovery, I thought of myself first as unworthy of love, then unlovable, and then hard to love. I was complicated and broken, and if people really knew me, I thought, then they wouldn't like me at all. Like my mother. She liked me sometimes, but she really didn't know me. This way of thinking about myself and relationships caused a lot of harm in my life and kept me tied to the psychache of my early years.

I think I knew that love, genuine love, would bring healing to the deeply broken places in me. It's part of why I gravitated to unhealthy relationships. Who would I be without the constant companion of pain? Whom would I court if not death? On the other hand, truly by God's grace, I never gave up. I also learned that I had value. God loved me and maybe that would be enough.

Finding the words to describe the years of searching for love and settling for less is proving to be difficult. I think of my first marriage and of so desperately wanting to be normal. When I was 24, my friends were all getting married, and I wanted that happiness, too. I wanted to prove to myself that I wasn't like my mother, so afraid of relationships that she chose unavailable men over and over again. Even on my wedding day, I knew I didn't want to marry the man who was waiting for me. I knew something was wrong, but I could not name it and I didn't trust myself enough to walk away. I thought God would make it okay. Marriage vows are sacred, right?

I spent two and a half years trying, trying, and trying some more, to find that happiness that newly married couples are supposed to have. I never did. I found divorce instead. I didn't know that no human shape could fill the void in me, could heal the psychache. So I kept trying. Shortly after my first marriage ended, I started dating a man 18 years older than I was. We laughed together and shared so much intensity, I thought I was in love. He seemed to value me. After an intense nine months, he ended our relationship while he was engulfed in depression, and married someone else two weeks later. I was crushed and wondered what was wrong with me. It didn't actually occur to me for quite some time that in this relationship the problem was not with me.

A few years later, I had grown up some. I had come to understand myself as a beloved child of God. I had forgiven myself for some of the choices I had made that resulted from my childhood. So when I came out and met a woman who seemed so full of life and who wanted to spend time with me, I thought I had finally figured it out. I could love and be loved! But I didn't have it quite right. When I lost my job in Harwich, I either had to move in with the woman I had been dating for a few months or return to my mother's house. Having just been rejected by the church and having no sense of sanctuary, there was no way I could move back to my childhood home.

Nine years later, I left that relationship. She had promised me so many things and none of them came to be. I left her house with what fit in my car. Walking away from each of my first two marriages are among the most courageous things I have ever done. But in the moment when I drove away—leaving the woman I had called my wife for several years, as well as my dogs and my cat—I felt only failure. I still could not find a fulltime call to ministry. The only church I had was the fledging Promise

Church, and its own status as an outcast did nothing to give me a sense of safety or hope for my future. *God may love me,* I thought, but no church wanted me, and marriage was something at which I had failed miserably—*twice.*

I didn't give up on either the church or relationships, though. I tried to find other work, without any luck. It turns out that even the secular nonprofits I approached couldn't see how my pastoral skills and experience could be beneficial. However, as far as relationships go, well, I was to discover that God has a fascinating sense of humor...

The short version is that, when I returned to seminary for a doctorate of ministry, I met a woman named Erika who first became my friend. I was very casually dating a man at the time and wasn't looking for romance. I was depressed and lost and trying to keep my life together. I could feel the pull of old wounds, tempting me to self-destruct. I didn't give in to that temptation any more than I could help, and my efforts were rewarded when I was hired to be the Clinical Chaplain at New Hampshire Hospital, the state psychiatric facility. This was my first fulltime job in a decade. The hospital did not particularly care about my personal life or my sexual identity.

Through my work at the hospital and my growing friendship with Erika, I started to find a true sense of myself. Yes, God loved me. Yes, *Erika* loved me. Yes, I could begin to love myself, even the parts I would rather not acknowledge. Gratitude flooded me unexpectedly in my first months of ministry at NHH. I started to be grateful for the hard times and the better times, for the church that initially saved me, for people such as John and Tim and Merle who saw me through the veil of darkness, for teachers and professors who tried to tell me how special I was, for therapists and spiritual directors who sat with me through the pain, for all the light God placed along my path. Mostly, as I learned to trust my ability to hold hope for those who could not hold it for themselves, I was grateful for those who had held that hope for me when I truly could not. There are no words to express the joy of finally knowing and believing that I am beloved.

The Power of Transformation

When I was in college, I read theology for the first time. I read Martin Luther, Paul Tillich, and Jürgen Moltmann.[2] Reading the writings of these theologians awoke something in me. I fell in love with this God who understood pain, this God who was in the depths as well as the heights. I wanted to know more and be the kind of person this God could love. I sought God in many places. I attended chapel services weekly, Thursday night Eucharist services, Christian Fellowship groups, and, at the end of my sophomore year, I began working as a youth coordinator for a large Presbyterian church nearby. I was on a quest.

One of the conservative Christian fellowship groups on campus pursued me to be on their leadership council. To be on the council, one had to tell one's faith journey to the paid staff person. I remember the day we walked around Muhlenberg's small campus while I told this woman my story as I understood it. I knew enough to add in a dramatic conversion story, which I placed neatly after my overdose. I alluded to my history of abuse and spoke openly about alcoholism in my family. She had some questions about when I met Christ and when I had been "saved," which I apparently answered to her satisfaction. Then, before we were supposed to pray, she looked at me and told me, "Everything happens according to God's will." She meant this to be comforting. To me, it was *horrifying!* How could all the things that had happened to me be God's will? I weighed her

---

2 I honestly don't remember the specific writings of Martin Luther that moved me back then. I remember feeling that his writings described a God who loved and wanted to be with God's people. From Luther I learned that God understood suffering in a deep and personal way. This was the beginning of my belief that God does not cause human suffering. At the same time, reading Tillich's *The Courage to Be* opened me to the idea of a God who lived and worked in and through human beings. If God were the ground of my being, as Tillich indicates, then there had to be more to me than all the misery I believed defined me. These ideas had their roots in Luther's and Tillich's works, but they were given life by Moltmann's *The Crucified God* and *The Theology of Joy*. The idea that we can meet God in our suffering was one that gave me tremendous hope as I struggled with my own pain. I also began a slow and tentative reach for the joy this same God could bring. I began to be able to envision a future free of psychache.

pronouncement against what I was learning in religion classes and decided that this woman was wrong; God did not make bad things happen. Though this decision effectively ended my involvement with that fellowship group, it was a step toward freedom for me.

Since those days, I've had an affinity for the Samaritan woman whom Jesus met at a well in the noonday sun (Jn. 4). Without a doubt, she was an outcast among outcasts, and she carried shame along with her jar as she came to draw water under the scorching sun. She also had a tenacity of spirit that whispers to my own. She who had had five husbands (plus one more man who wasn't her husband) was not unclean or untouchable to Jesus' way of thinking. For him, she was infinitely worth saving. He risked the scorn of his followers to talk with this unclean woman in the middle of the day. He was breaking rules and stepping into impropriety. Jesus did not care about that. In this woman who carried on under the weight of her experiences he saw only a woman beautiful and whole, on whom he would pour living water. With his love, unconditionally offered, he transformed her from outcast to prophet.

The power of this story brings tears to my eyes every time. Some are tears of sadness for all the times I as a minister of the gospel have failed to do the same for others, for all the times the church as the embodiment of Christ has failed to do the same, and for all those who thirst and don't believe there is a well where they can go to draw the water of life. Other tears are of joy: joy that the Spirit pursued me until I came to the well, joy that I have been able to let the same Spirit use me to lead others to the well, and joy that as long as there is thirst there will be a well of living water.

I sometimes wonder what would have become of that woman if Jesus hadn't decided to stop for a drink that day. I know what would have happened to me if John and that congregation in Hyannis hadn't thought I was worth stopping for. I have long credited John and that church with saving my life. Only recently, though, have I come see that *this is what church needs to be about* all *the time.* We, the church, have the power of the Holy Spirit in our midst...and we spend our time worrying about growing our numbers and balancing our budgets. These things cannot be more important than saving lives—one at a time, if need be.

Setting aside all issues of theology and doctrine, we, the church, need to be united in the effort to save people's lives. Spiritual salvation is meaningless when people are killing themselves—either outright, or slowly with addictions, eating disorders, and self-harming behaviors. The only cure for psychache is unconditional love. We, the church, know this. To all people who wonder just who they really are, we, the church, should be proclaiming, "You are beloved children of God!" To all who wonder where they belong, we, the church, should be opening wide our doors in welcome, saying, "You belong here in this loving, faithful community of God's beloved."

In effect, this is what my childhood church said to me. This is what John's consistent presence said to me. This message of unconditional love that, for years, I did not consciously hear or feel was nonetheless able to sustain me until most of the broken places were healed and I could see the truth that had been there all along. The pain in my life was not God's doing. While I thought God didn't love me because God did nothing to prevent the horrible things that happened to me, I later came to see that God kept putting people in my path who led me through the darkness. Even the fact that I knew from early on that my eating disorder was unhealthy and self-destructive was a gift from God.[3] Like the Samaritan woman at the well, I have been blessed with a tenacity of spirit that prevented me from giving up during all the years when living was so hard. Also like that unnamed Samaritan woman, I was fortunate enough to encounter Christ at a time when I felt as if I was beyond humanity's reach.

---

3 My experiences as a pastor and therapist confirmed what I heard while I was in treatment for my eating disorder. Many people in the early stages of an eating disorder—and often in the later ones, too—will adamantly defend their right to starve themselves. The statement I have most frequently heard is, "It's my body and I can do what I want with it." For Christians, particularly, this is a fallacy. Scripture clearly states that our bodies belong to God and are on loan to us as a dwelling place, a temple, of the Holy Spirit (1 Cor. 6:19–20).

Self, Neighbor, Creation, and God

During the week that I was in the hospital after my overdose, I kept saying that I did not want to be alone. I had no other words to express how I felt. As much as I wouldn't have thought it possible, I felt more alone after I tried to kill myself than before. Though people came to visit, it wasn't the literal company of people I needed. I needed to feel *connected* in a way that I could not even begin to express when I was 15. My mother misunderstood what I meant and made sure that I was not alone for the school vacation week that followed my discharge. Being with people—caring people, for sure—became more exhausting than being alone. Finally, I begged for a day by myself. My mother was exasperated. She thought she was doing what I had asked.

That sense of aloneness I experienced then haunted me for many years. It was evidence of what I later called the "anorexic paradox," a profound fear of what is most needed. I most needed to feel connected to a person or a community as an equal, a welcomed participant, even as I was extremely fearful of just that. It took decades before I finally rid myself of the idea that if people really knew me, they would not like me. I always held something in reserve; I never did anything 100 percent, so that if I failed I could say that I didn't do my best anyway. But the longing to belong somewhere, to be a part of something, persisted for years.

Even in the congregation that cared so much for me as a child, there was no space to talk about the hard times. They were there for me, yes, and probably would have remained present even if I had not recovered well. Yet, when I decided to go to seminary at age 22, the congregation was anxious to hear the details and made no mention of my recent past. In fact, I was advised by both pastors not to talk about it, to put it behind me and simply show the various committees that I was healthy and ready to respond to God's call.

For decades, I heeded those words. I didn't talk about my past experience with suicide, suicidal thoughts, depression, or eating disorder. None of it. I didn't mention the times when I struggled with depression after relationships ended and old wounds were re-opened. I seldom acknowledged that I had eating-disorder thoughts when I felt rejected or abandoned or helpless. I certainly never spoke about the passive suicidality, the thought that if I went to sleep and did not wake up, that would be okay with me, even though that would recur for years. Somehow, I knew that the church I loved would not be comfortable with any of this information. It didn't matter whether I was pastor or parishioner. The Body of Christ becomes anxious when such things are named, forgetting that we are one, forgetting that if one member is struggling the whole Body struggles.

I decided to put an end to this silence and challenge the church to find ways of acknowledging, accepting, and making room for those who live with psychache or mental illness. During my years as a clinical chaplain, I had opportunities to educate congregations and clergy on the topic of mental illness, to remove some of the stigma people carry. In addition, I started working with the State Suicide Prevention Council. I realized how ill-prepared most clergy are to respond to people who are experiencing a mental health crisis, let alone people who are suicidal. When did we, the Body of Christ, forget that so many who struggle with depression and mental illness want and need to be included, welcomed, known, and loved? When did we forget that we are to care for those who are unable to care for themselves?

Henri Nouwen writes beautifully about being God's beloved in *Life of the Beloved*.[4] He understood the power of depression, and he also understood quite well the power of love to bring hope and healing. Our call is to embody Christ—literally to embody *Holy Love*. If we do this, no one individual's psychache, illness, despair, addiction, or pain of any kind should be avoided by the church. If we embody Christ, then we love as Christ loves, and we know how freely Jesus offered hope and healing to all who came to him. This is how Nouwen puts it:

> When we claim and constantly reclaim the truth of being chosen ones, we soon discover within ourselves a deep desire to reveal to others their own chosenness. Instead of making us feel that we are better, more precious or valuable than others, our awareness of being chosen opens

---

4 Henri J. M. Nouwen, *Life of the Beloved* (New York: Crossroads, 1992).

our eyes to the chosenness of others. That is the great joy of being chosen: the discovery that others are chosen as well. In the house of God there are many mansions. There is a place for everyone—a unique, special place. Once we deeply trust that we ourselves are precious in God's eyes, we are able to recognize the preciousness of others and their unique places in God's heart.[5]

The problem I have discovered in my journey toward wholeness and in accompanying others on theirs is that very few people truly believe they have a unique place in God's heart. In all our striving toward Christian perfection, we seem to have forgotten the original message—God so loves the whole of the cosmos (Jn. 3:16). Love we have aplenty. When will we claim it and believe it for ourselves and share it unreservedly with all God's children?

What Your Congregation Can Do Now:

- Recognize the power of words and welcome. Is your congregation truly welcoming of all people? How do you convey that welcome explicitly?

- Seek to be a congregation that values saving lives above all else.

- Create an atmosphere of welcome and hospitality through words and actions that affirm the value of individuals.

- Put supports in place for those who might feel vulnerable during worship and need companionship.

---

5 Ibid., 63–64.

Chapter 6

The Body of Christ
Is Broken...*and* Whole

When you pass through the waters, I will be with you;
and through the rivers, they shall not overwhelm you;
when you walk through fire you shall not be burned,
and the flame shall not consume you.

—Isaiah 43:2

I found redemption in the strangest place: a state psychiatric hospital. I had been a pastor and a therapist, yet the place I found the most healing was the psych hospital. For the first time in my life I could draw fully on all the painful experiences I had had, and could offer genuine hope to the patients there. I could assure them of God's love for them because I was sure of God's love for me. I could tell them that there would be joy amidst the pain, because I had been in pain and experienced times of joy. While I knew that many of the patients in the hospital would have lifetime battles with severe and persistent mental illness, I also knew beyond a doubt that they were beloved children of God and deserved to be treated that way.

There were days when it was hard to bear witness to such suffering and to hold onto hope of any kind. There were days that were exhausting and overwhelming. But, then, there were moments of such profound grace that my life has been forever

61

changed. There is no experience like leading worship with those patients. Each week we would go through the usual liturgy and share communion. I hardly have words for what it felt like to join in prayers of confession with those who gathered in that small chapel, knowing some of the heinous crimes some of them had committed. Then to pronounce words of absolution. Never have I felt the mantle of priestly duty so heavily...or welcomed it with such gratitude. Each week I stood and said the words, "Hear the Good News: In Christ you are forgiven. In Christ you are set free to live as the whole people of God." I said those words, and I had to mean them. They were true for me and for all who gathered in that small chapel.

If that wasn't enough, offering bread and wine to people who were so broken—some of whom had raped, murdered, or committed other acts of violence while they were psychotic—made my own theology very real. To offer the Bread of Life and the Cup of Salvation and say, "Given for you," made me realize that Christ did exactly that. He offered his body and blood to save us from ourselves, to save us from isolation, and to bind us together into a loving community: Christ's own body. The last shreds of my own self-rejection and resistance to forgiveness disappeared during those worship services.

In those years, I came to understand a verse in Romans that had never made much sense to me before: "We know that all things work together for good for those who love God, who are called according to [God's] purpose" (Rom. 8:28). It isn't that God causes bad things to happen to test us or punish us. It's simply that bad things happen in a world that is far from perfect, a world in which random things happen like mental illness, cancer, and earthquakes. Additionally, people make spectacularly bad choices and end up hurting undeserving, innocent people around them. However, eventually goodness comes out of even the worst human experiences. Working at the hospital helped me understand this for myself and for many of the patients who were able to find healing even when there was no cure.

Putting Our Fingers in the Wounds

If reading Luther, Tillich, and Moltmann in college opened the possibility of a God who knows and experiences pain, then reading Henri Nouwen's *The Wounded Healer*[1] in seminary gave me hope that my own pain could be transformed and, possibly, allow me to connect with other people in a genuine way. Of course, it took me years before I accepted this as reality. I had a tendency to view my life as either/or, when it is most often both/and. I was either wounded or whole, anorexic or recovered, straight or gay. When I learned to see the myriad colors between black and white on the colorful spectrum of my life, I could accept the possibility of my own woundedness being shaped into a gift.

The truth against which I had struggled for so long is that I have scars, some of them very deep. Most of the wounds are healed, but they ache some days just as a physical injury might. It's okay that they ache, for they remind me of where I have been, where some people still live, and where I am now. The scars, even when they ache, do not detract from the whole person I am or the person I continue to become. Perhaps I am like those Japanese bowls mended with gold, my own mended places making me more beautiful, more unique.

Another truth is that I no longer have an eating disorder. However, when some of those old wounds ache, my thinking becomes skewed and I feel I could easily be pulled into self-destructive behaviors again. I've learned that I need to tell someone I trust when I become tangled in these thoughts. Speaking the truth out loud breaks the spell my thinking can create. There's a reason Jesus is the Word become flesh...

Another truth is that I am bisexual. When I first figured out that I was attracted to women, I thought that was it. I was a lesbian and that explained some of my relationship difficulties. Well, you might imagine my surprise when I found myself attracted to a man after my second marriage ended. I used to think, like many people, that when someone identified as bisexual they were just avoiding the reality of being attracted to the same gender. How wrong I was! Being bisexual for me means that I am attracted to a gender identity that crosses the midsection between male and female. I should have known that *this*, too, would be a case of both/and.

All of this and more that I haven't included contributes to my wounded places. Even on the days now when all I feel is the old

---

1 Henri Nouwen, *The Wounded Healer* (New York: Doubleday, 1972).

ache, I have hope. I think of Thomas and his encounter with the resurrected Christ. Thomas wouldn't believe until he saw Jesus' wounds for himself. Then, when Jesus appeared with Thomas in the room, Jesus held up his hands and invited Thomas to touch the wound in his side. Jesus as the Risen Christ identified himself to his disciples by his wounds! Why don't we pay more attention to this? Jesus wasn't ashamed of his wounds; they were part of his human and divine experience. If you want to know Christ, you cannot deny his wounds. If you want to know yourself, don't deny yours.

It's true. If nothing else, the Body of Christ today is wounded and, in some places, wounded deeply. I wonder what would happen if one day everyone who was in worship identified their wounds. If everyone who had experienced abuse, violence, carried a mental health diagnosis, battled addiction, contemplated or engaged in suicidal behavior, or had any other kind of trauma stood up, who would remain seated? Not me. Not anyone.

The Body of Christ is wounded, and, in its woundedness, is made whole. Jesus' life and ministry was about healing, liberation, and restoration. When we come together to worship, we cannot leave our wounds on the doorstep; they come in with us. Sometimes we are brave enough to let others see our pain. Most of the time, we come to worship and keep our pain to ourselves. Next time you pass the "Peace of Christ," think of it as lovingly touching the wounded places in those who share that worship space with you. Maybe you could even have the courage to imagine others' hands just as lovingly touching your own wounds. Will this change how you see church? Wounded, yet together in Christ, made whole? Therefore, no taboo subjects should remain, not even suicide.

Emotional Freedom

When I worked at New Hampshire Hospital, I led many groups. One of the frequent topics of those groups was emotions. I knew from both personal and professional experience that feelings are challenging, and we make judgments about which are "good" and which are "bad." Many people, even those outside a psychiatric hospital, have trouble naming their emotions, even when they experience them. I used to start one group by having participants name as many feelings as they could. Usually, it started off slowly and took some prodding, but they could usually name fifty—and, sometimes, more than a hundred—different emotions. Then we would move on to talking about the ones we liked and ones we didn't like. And the ones that got us into difficulty.

Anger was always the one that was a problem. People do things in anger that they wouldn't normally do. If you are experiencing symptoms of mental illness, then you likely have less ability to keep impulses in check. So we would take a closer look at anger since it was so troublesome. I would ask how long the most intense feelings of anger last, and always the group would agree that it wasn't more than five or ten minutes of intense, seemingly uncontrollable anger. We would then spend the rest of the group time talking about noticing anger before it took over and how to cope effectively with uncomfortable feelings. Inevitably, someone would say that simply paying attention to their breathing could get a person through anything that only lasted five or ten minutes. This insight helped remind us that we don't have to act on the feelings we have, and we don't have to feel bad for having them.

From these groups, I have created a children's sermon about being able to bring all of our feelings to God—even the ones we don't like, and maybe especially the ones that get us into trouble. I draw various emoticons and ask the kids to name them, and then divide them into "good" and "bad." Then I talk about how God loves us no matter what feelings we have. We can name them and feel them, but we don't have to act on them. Then I am always careful to place all the feelings on the altar or communion table. It's an important message: God loves the fullness of our humanity, not just the "good" parts.

When I was installed at the Presbyterian church I served as an associate pastor, the woman who gave the charge said, "To be an effective pastor, you need to be willing and able to share your whole self with the congregation." I was somewhat horrified by her words because I did not understand what she meant. There were boundaries, were there not? Years later, long after I had left that congregation, I realized what a gift she had tried to give me that day. To share my whole self with a congregation simply meant to bring the fullness of my humanity to my ministry, scars and all, in a way that would invite the congregation to do the same.

I long for the day when prayer requests in all congregations honor the fullness of our humanity and trust that God's grace and mercy are enough to cover all. I imagine a day when it is acceptable for someone to say during the sharing of joys and concerns, "Please pray for me today, I'm having suicidal thoughts," or, "Please pray for me today because I feel lost and alone," or, "Please pray for me today because I feel hopeless." We already find it pretty easy to pray for people who have challenges to their physical health, and people usually offer these requests freely. Why are we not praying just as freely and openly about mental and spiritual health concerns? It is well past time for the Body of Christ to bear one another's burdens truly and fully.

What Your Congregation Can Do Now:

- Recognize the healing and community-shaping power in sharing the sacrament of communion.

- Practice passing the "Peace of Christ" with intention.

- Practice voicing and hearing prayer concerns for mental health challenges.

- Work toward being a community that invites honesty and authenticity.

- Practice gratitude for the gifts of the whole community, and the individual members.

- Improve systems of congregational care to ensure that the most vulnerable are cared for by many members of the congregation.

Chapter 7

The Body of Christ Is a Lifesaver

So then, putting away falsehood, let all of us speak the truth to our neighbors, for we are members of one another.
—Ephesians 4:25

After I "came out" and experienced such profound rejection by the church, I tried to leave it. Always, I was pulled back in because I had come to believe that God loved me even if the church did not. Sometimes it was very hard to hold onto a sense of God's love for me. Once, I was asked to be a short-term interim for a congregation that had already rejected my application to be their settled pastor. Another time, a search committee chose me to be their candidate for settled pastor only to have the church be packed with inactive members who went so far as to say, "She's a good preacher and probably a good pastor, but we don't want her because she's gay." They were so steadfast in their convictions that my family and I had to be escorted out of the building for our own safety.

One of the worst things any congregation can do is cause harm to an individual in the name of God. I've never understood how churches can justify messages of hatred and condemnation when they claim to be followers of Christ. Yet, so many churches feel justified in judging, condemning, and casting out individuals and whole groups of people for perceived sins. I wonder how many lives have been lost because a congregation has acted hatefully and claimed to do so on God's behalf. How many people have died by suicide believing that God hates them because the church told them so?

As previously mentioned, during the decade after I came out, I was unable to find a permanent fulltime call to parish ministry. While I do not regret the years I spent as a therapist and as the gathering pastor of Promise Church, the pain I experienced during those years was unnecessary. We, too often, make the mistake of forgetting that the church is made up of human beings and, as such, sometimes gets things wrong. The church has been wrong in its reaction to LGBTQ+ people, to people with mental illness, to perpetrators and victims of domestic violence, to people with developmental disabilities, and many others, including women and persons living with HIV/AIDS. I feel deep pain when I think of how many people have been turned away from church and told they are unworthy, unwanted, unloved. This is not embodying Christ. This is not saving lives.

It's time the church stopped worshiping its own peculiar interpretations of the Bible and resumed worshiping the Living Word. Dorothy Soelle suggests that Jesus has many followers and few friends.[1] She also describes Jesus, and those who would be his friends, as *goel* (witness-redeemer). This is the job of the church, the Body of Christ: to bear witness to suffering and create space for healing and redemption. Anytime one who claims the name of Christ yet acts without love, anytime a church rejects or condemns, then they are not embodying Christ. If it is not love, then it is not the way of Christ.

When I was 15 and actively suicidal, no one knew that I was thinking about killing myself for a long time before the day I acted on impulse and swallowed a bunch of pills. It's easy for me to say in hindsight that someone should have known something and done something to get me help, but in those days no one talked openly about depression, eating disorders, or abuse. How was anyone to know what was going in my head if I could not tell them? The important thing is that when people found out, especially church people, they did everything they knew how to do to communicate their love and support of me. No one told me

---

1   Dorothy Soelle, *Choosing Life* (Eugene, Oreg.: Wipf & Stock, 2003).

I was going to hell for wanting to die. No one told me to "just get over it." They offered only love and support. Granted, they had no idea how to respond as my eating disorder became worse, but what they did was welcome me when I showed up. In John's case, he continued to meet with me regularly to try to understand and to help bear my pain.

It was this early experience of church being church at its best that led me to ordained ministry. It was also what held me through the years of rejection by the same church that ordained me. I had learned that church at its best is the embodiment of Christ's love, and that church at its worst is an embodiment of every human fear. It has been the source of healing and the source of pain for me. It's another instance of both/and, and it has taken me a long time to come to terms with that. The truth of the matter is that the church can be very godly and bring healing. It can also be incredibly self-righteous and bring pain. In either case, the church is people doing their best to embody the Christ they know. Sometimes, the Christ of the church is far too small, and much more a reflection of the fearful souls who gather there than an embodiment of Christ's largesse.

Even so, as church membership continues to dwindle, we cannot continue to ignore the gospel call. It's a simple one, really: "Love your neighbor as yourself" (Mk. 12:31, Mt. 22:39). Or, put more directly: as Jesus said to his disciples, "Love one another as I have loved you" (Jn. 13:34–35). The mandate of scripture is clear: we are to care for one another, especially those who are vulnerable and cannot care for themselves. This is the true work of the church. Yes, we need to worship to remind ourselves that God is God and we are not, and to express our gratitude for the blessings we receive each day. Yes, we need to study the Scriptures so that the Word continues to come alive and challenge us. However, if we are not engaged in caring for the most vulnerable among us, then we are not doing the work of Christ.

I doubt that the church in Hyannis understood their care for me as embodying Christ or doing Christ's work. They did what they did because I was a child of that church. They knew me and they cared and they did not want to see me in pain. I wonder how many others they have saved and how many others, whom they did not know, walked out of their doors and into their own unbearable pain. It's time we stop worrying about who's a member and who is not, and reach outside our sanctuaries to bring healing where it is needed. We can all be better neighbors—which brings us back to creating community that clearly demonstrates everyone belongs and everyone is loved.

The True Power of the Gospel

When I worked at the psychiatric hospital, one of the most common questions people asked me was, "How does God feel about suicide?" Without exception, the people asking wanted to kill themselves, but were afraid that God would condemn them for it. It did not matter what I thought about God's view of suicide, what mattered was the person asking the question. My answer to this question is, "God is not a fan of suicide." Often, I had to explain this, because someone wanting to kill themselves wants evidence. They believe that their life is their own and they can do with it as they want. If I thought otherwise, I had to prove it. Depression, psychosis, PTSD, or psychache often convince the sufferer that the world would be better off without them in it. It is hard to break through this illusion created by pain. However, I continued to engage each of these persons in conversation that went something like this:

> **Me:** Do you believe that God created life?
> **Patient:** Yes.
> **Me:** Do you believe that God gave you the gift of your life?
> **Patient:** Yes. But I don't like it and I don't want it anymore.
> **Me:** Do you want to tell God that God's gift to you isn't good enough?
> **Patient:** Well, no.
> **Me:** Then you see what I mean when I say that God is not a fan of suicide?
> **Patient:** Yes. God wants me to keep the life I have.
> **Me:** Right. Should we talk about ways of dealing with the pain so you don't want to die?
> **Patient:** I guess…

My own personal belief about God and suicide is not relevant when I am attempting to save a life and offer hope. Many mainline Protestants are quick to jump in with reassurance that God loves and forgives everyone, no matter what. On the other hand, many Catholics and more conservative Protestants tend to believe that if a person dies by suicide, they are damned. This belief harkens back to days before psychology gave us insight into the many ways in which the human mind can be tortured. Even the official stance of the Catholic Church is one that leans toward mercy.[2] However, to one contemplating suicide, belief that they will "go to hell" may be the only thing stopping them from suicide. Until other protective factors—belonging to a community, feeling loved, recognizing one's own value—can be strengthened, it is unwise to change this belief.

Yet it is equally foolish to allow survivors of suicide loss to hold tightly to the belief of God's condemnation. There is no biblical evidence that those who die by suicide are condemned to eternity away from God's presence. There are seven instances of suicide in the Bible[3] and not one of them mentions God's response. Any theology that claims absolute surety of God's response bases its claim on conjecture. One who suffers the loss of a loved one to suicide is potentially at risk for suicide themselves if they believe that their loved one will be alone in hell forever. In this situation, I always point out God's acts of love and mercy and suggest the possibility that God will be understanding and merciful toward their loved one. However, there is no way of knowing. Those of us who believe in a loving, merciful God err on the side of

---

2 Paragraphs 2282 and 2283 of Part 3, Chapter 2, Article 5 in the *Catechism of the Catholic Church* state respectively: "Grave psychological disturbances, anguish, or grave fear of hardship, suffering, or torture can diminish the responsibility of the one committing suicide," and, "We should not despair of the eternal salvation of persons who have taken their own lives. By ways known to him alone, God can provide the opportunity for salutary repentance. The Church prays for persons who have taken their own lives." http://www.vatican.va/archive/ccc_css/archive/catechism/p3s2c2a5.htm

3 Biblical references to suicide: Abimelech (Judg. 9:54), Samson (Judg. 16:30), Saul (1 Chron. 10:4), Saul's armor-bearer (1 Chron. 10:5), Ahithophel (2 Sam. 17:23), Zimri (1 Kings 16:18), and Judas (Mt. 27:5).

forgiveness, grace, and peace. Those of us who believe in a God who passes judgment err on the side of condemnation. This is why, when asked, I always say, diplomatically, that God is not a fan of suicide. Everything I know about God says that God's heart is broken anytime anyone takes their own life, whatever the circumstances.

When the church saved my life at 15, I thought I would always have a safe place. When the church rejected me at 31, I wondered whether I would ever feel safe again. Years of heartache passed before I could see that God rejoices when we embody love for one another, and God's own heart breaks when we fail. Contemplating the heart of God always leads me to the communion table.

Jesus was intimately acquainted with humanity's capacity for betrayal and nonetheless he gathered with his friends and disciples in that upper room. He ate with them, laughed with them, cried with them, sang with them, and prayed with them. Then he *offered himself* to them, in spite of—or, because of—what would follow. "This is my body broken for you. This is my blood, the new covenant, poured out for the forgiveness of sins." We hear these words. Yet we do not actually *hear* them. There is no one for whom Christ's body was not broken; remember that Judas was at that table in the upper room. No one is excluded from the new covenant that binds us with forgiveness in communities of love. Yet we often fail to hear the message of inclusion, forgiveness, and grace!

Spirituality, Religion, and Healing the Psychache

"There is a balm in Gilead to heal the sin sick soul"[4] is one of my favorite lines from the old hymns. Jesus is the balm that heals the pain of sin. Today, the church is the embodiment of Christ. Today, the church is the balm that heals the pain of sin and psychache. We are often blind to this power we have in our midst. The power that raised Christ from the dead that first Easter morning, that set holy heads on fire on Pentecost, and that gathered followers of the Way is the very same power that

4 "There Is a Balm in Gilead" is a traditional African American Spiritual of unknown authorship.

creates and sustains the church today. We, as the church, have the power to save lives, maybe even pull them from the grips of death. I know this to be true because it is my story. You've read it in these pages. Moreover, I am not the only one who can tell this kind of story that moves from the hell of the void and the pain of psychache into the joyful life of the Spirit. Will we remember whose we are when we gather each week to worship, to pray, to sing praises to God? And will we re-member those who are left out of our kinship? *If we are not sharing the power of the Spirit to save lives, we are not church.*

Somewhere in my family's photo albums there is a picture of me at age eight or nine. I am reaching up to the sky as if to shake God's hand. My parents and others often asked what I was doing in the picture, and I never told them. When it was taken, I was at a party given by friends of my father. They were baptizing people in their pool, but would not baptize me. They told me, kindly enough, that I had already been baptized and already belonged to God. The man who took my picture told me that all I had to do was reach up and take God's hand. I did reach up. I just had no idea that God took my hand—had, in fact, *already* been holding it. It took me a lifetime to be comfortable in God's strong, wounded, beautiful hands. Longer, still, before I realized that my hands were also strong, wounded, and beautiful, and could be used to save lives.

It's hard in a society that wants easy, comfortable answers. If we feel badly, we want a pill to fix it. If we pray, we want instant answers. If we are sick, we want immediate cures. We are impatient and we have forgotten the joy of an intimate relationship with God. We want spirituality without the trappings of religion. While I agree that church can be far too heavy-handed with its dogma and doctrine, spirituality that isn't anchored in any faith tradition often leaves a person floating out in the universe, feeling disconnected and without a sense of belonging. In addition, without faith, psychache can flourish.

We, as human beings, need faith communities. I am clearly Christian, so I will say we need church. Studies have shown that people who are active in faith communities have better health outcomes. They live longer. They recover more quickly from illness. They are happier with their quality of life.[5] People have become skeptical of religion because churches have clung to traditions and theologies that predate science and technology. If we want to be the lifesaving communities we were intended to be, then we must let go of anything that is not essential for Christian faith in this moment. We must trust the God who led the Israelites through the desert, the God who asked a teenage girl to be the one to bear God into the world, the God who conquered death, the God who led Peter and Paul far beyond any place they could have predicted, the God whose church survives thousands of years later... We must trust this God. We must trust this God to show us how to be the fullest embodiment of Christ we can be, to show us how to be a church that saves lives.

At this point, I would be remiss if I did not say that the church alone, no matter how healthy it is or how fully it embodies Christ, cannot take the place of medical or psychiatric or psychological treatment for one who suffers from mental illness or addictions. Congregations can support wellness and recovery by providing a loving place, a place of acceptance and belonging and inclusion. Sometimes, being a part of a community gives someone courage to reach out for treatment because they know they are loved and supported and valued. Sometimes, knowing that people are praying for you and holding hope for you is enough to keep trying when nothing seems to be helping you to feel better.

While I have mentioned hospitalization, therapy, and spiritual direction along my own journey toward recovery, I haven't said anything about medication. The summer I was at Boston Children's hospital for eating disorder treatment, I was prescribed an antidepressant, and I had an adverse reaction to two different types. While I was in my thirties, I was again prescribed an antidepressant, and had a bad reaction to that as well. Because of these reactions and other allergies, I've had to find a way to manage the symptoms of depression without benefit of medication. I wouldn't wish this on anyone. Mental illnesses

---

5 Harold Koenig's work addresses the connection between religious practice and health outcomes with profound clarity. For a summary of his work in this area, see Harold Koenig, Dana King, and Verna B. Carson, *Handbook of Religion and Health, 2nd Edition* (Oxford: Oxford University Press, 2012).

are diseases of the brain, physical illnesses, and ought to be treated as such. The church cannot replace physical or psychiatric treatment for depression and other mental health challenges, but it can make the difference between simply *surviving* and truly *living*.

There is, indeed, a balm in Gilead. It's you and me and the Christ who works in and through us. Together we can become the lifesaving church. We can embody Christ and, in so doing, help prevent suicide.

What Your Congregation Can Do Now:

- Be mindful that saving lives is the primary work of the church.

- Model Christ in the inclusion, welcome, and re-membering of each person who comes in the door.

- Be attentive to the power of the Holy Spirit to lead you in unexpected directions of healing and wholeness.

- Share in the sacred ritual of communion with the understanding that sometimes we sit in Judas' seat, and yet are still welcome at Christ's table (meaning Jesus welcomes all who seek forgiveness and healing in his body, broken, and the cup poured out).

- Continue to educate yourselves on how the congregation can become a lifesaving congregation by understanding better the role congregations play in recovery from mental health challenges as well as in suicide prevention, intervention, and postvention. (See Appendix C: Resources for Laypeople.)

The Big Questions

Is Suicide Preventable?

I expect that some of you have read through this book hoping to have some questions answered. One of them is the question of prevention. While those of us who work in the field of suicidology have been heard to say that suicide is 100 percent preventable, this statement is somewhat misleading. We should probably say that we are working toward a day when suicide is 100 percent preventable, or that suicide could be 100 percent preventable. As it is now, there is so much stigma and so much shame around suicidality that people often mask and deny their thoughts and plans of suicide. If we continue to work to remove the stigma, then prevention becomes more likely. We have a long way to go.

In the meantime, those who are survivors of suicide loss need to be assured that they are not to blame. The sense of, "If only I had...," or, "Why didn't I...?" can be devastating. There is no way to know what is truly in the mind of another. Having been one who could have died by suicide and who then hid her subsequent suicidality for years, I can honestly say that sometimes we just don't know what another person is going through. It is not our fault for not knowing if a friend or family member hid their struggles well, or if they suicided on an impulse. There are no words that can ease the pain of this kind of guilt, but that is no reason to remain silent. I will keep saying that survivors are not to blame. (See Appendix E: Resources for Suicide Loss Survivors.)

However, I will also say that we need to be aware of the signs and symptoms that indicate that someone is at risk for suicide. (See Appendix A: Signs of Suicide Risk.) If you think someone is at risk, don't be afraid to ask. You will not cause someone to suicide just by asking. In fact, you may literally save a life. We can work toward removing the shame and stigma that leads people to remain silent and isolated as they struggle with suicidality. It is possible that one day, all suicides may be preventable. Let's keep the conversation going.

Is Suicide a Sin?

Is suicide a sin? This, of course, is the big question that many readers were hoping I would answer. Yes, suicide is a sin, but not in the way you may think. As I have clearly stated, I believe that God is not a fan of suicide, though I believe God is merciful. However, if sin is a break in relationship with self, with neighbor, with creation, or with God, then suicide meets that definition of sin on several fronts.

However, I don't believe that the sin lies with the individual suffering from psychache. The real sin lies with the Body of Christ. It is this Body of Christ, the church, that commits sin when suicide takes place. We have broken relationship with ourselves and our neighbor (as with one, so with all). We have also broken relationship with God, who asks that we embody love. This is the real sin of suicide: that someone has remained outside the reaches of God's love. We have failed to save a life by not including someone. We have not lived into the fullness of the gospel; the individual who suicided did not know that God's realm is right here, right now, waiting to fill them with an abundance of grace, love, and healing.

If the individual who is suicidal has any part in the sin, it is that they deny they are loved by God and their life has value. Of course, there are many, many reasons for this for which the individual may not be responsible, but the break in relationship, the sin, remains present. And again, the Body of Christ may bear more responsibility for this sin than the individual who suffers.

I realize that this isn't a comforting answer to the question, and you may not even find it helpful. There is hope, however. Scripture tells us that there is only one unforgiveable sin (Mk. 3:28–29), and suicide is not it. Whatever "blasphemy against the Holy Spirit" is, it isn't suicide. This means that the communal sin surrounding suicide can be forgiven. We also know that Jesus often told those whom he healed to, "Go, and sin no more," or, "Go and do not sin again." This is our challenge. As the Body of Christ, we must endeavor not to repeat our sin of failing to save a life. We must break the silence around suicidality and self-harm. We must be willing to face into the void and the pain of psychache with those who suffer, and be willing to embody a love that is patient, steadfast, and without condition.

Signs of Suicide Risk

There are many factors that contribute to suicidality. There is no singular cause, but there are changes in conversation, behavior, or mood that can indicate higher risk.

If a person expresses any of the following, they may be at risk for suicide:

- being in intolerable pain and wanting it to end

- feeling trapped by life in general or specific circumstances

- not able to see that life has meaning or that they have a reason to live

- a sense that others would be better off without them

- wanting to die, wanting to suicide, or thinking about suicide

If a person engages in any of the following, they may be at risk for suicide:

- increase in or excessive use of alcohol or drugs

- engaging in high risk or potentially life-threatening behaviors

- making contact with people just to say "goodbye" (phone call, text, email, etc.)

- giving away valued possessions

- a significant change in sleeping patterns (sleeping too much or too little)

- an increase in aggression

- isolating themselves from loved ones

- dropping out of previously enjoyed activities

- openly looking for access to means to suicide (e.g., through internet searches, conversations, etc.)

Mood changes that may indicate a risk for suicide include:

- new or worsening depression (while new or worsening depression increases a person's risk for suicide, a person might also be at higher risk if they have been discharged from a hospital stay for depression or other mood disorders)

- new or increased anxiety

- a deep sense of shame and/or guilt

- intense anger or rage

- isolation

If you think someone is at risk for suicide, ask them if they have thoughts of suicide, a plan, and means to follow through. If the person acknowledges having thoughts but does not have a plan or means, then try to assist them in finding appropriate professional help. If a person confirms having thoughts and a plan but is without means, the risk may be higher. You may want to seek help more urgently. If the person has thoughts, plans, and means, you may need to accompany them to the nearest emergency department or call 9-1-1 if they refuse. These are guidelines, meant to help you respond appropriately to identified risk. However, people are not always honest, and if you believe a person is at imminent risk for suicide, then calling emergency services is the best option. If you are right, you may have helped save a life. If you are wrong, and the person is angry with you, better to have them alive and angry than to deal with the aftermath of suicide. If you are uncertain, call a psychologist, clinical social worker, or therapist to get more advice. You can find these people by searching online or looking up your local suicide prevention agency. You may also find useful information online at https://afsp.org/ (American Foundation for Suicide Prevention).

Resources for Clergy

The Moral and Ethical Responsibility

As I suggested in chapter 4, I believe that all clergy have a moral and ethical responsibility to respond to suicide in ways that are least likely to contribute to contagion or copycat behavior. This is not as easy as any of us would like it to be. We would like to be able to say without qualifiers that suicide is either a sin or it is not. We would like to be able to offer something definitive to those struggling with suicidality and those who survive suicide loss. The fact is that we cannot. You may not like my response that says, "God is not a fan of suicide," without answering the question of sin or salvation. That's okay. It just means that you will have to come up with your own answer.

Let's start with theology. Generally speaking, if you are affiliated with a more traditional or conservative denomination, you are more likely to believe that one who dies by suicide is beyond redemption. In other words: that person will go to hell. Similarly, if you belong to a more liberal or progressive denomination, you more likely believe that suicide does not exclude a person from God's love and salvation. I've already indicated some of the concerns with both sets of belief. (See pages 70-72.) Both sets of belief have the potential to cause harm and to increase the risk of more suicides. The bottom line is that the Bible says nothing about God's response to suicide, so all our theologies are conjecture. This does not make one side right and the other wrong. It does serve as a reminder that saving lives isn't necessarily about what we as individuals believe, or necessarily what our denomination endorses. It comes down to the needs and beliefs of the people involved.

When it comes to assessing suicide risk, clinicians do so, in part, by evaluating protective and risk factors. Protective factors are just what you think they are. They are strengths of the individual that contribute to the likelihood that the person will not suicide. These can include things like: strong connections with family or friends, positive engagement with community groups, solid work history, pursuit of hobbies, active faith life, and other life-supporting activities and belief systems. Not surprisingly, risk factors are those things that detract from a healthy quality of life and may include: difficult relationships with family or friends, divorce, grief, prolonged physical illness, abuse history, addictions, disconnection from community groups, loss of support systems, faith beliefs that emphasize judgment and shame, and other things that leave a person feeling hurt, isolated, and worthless.

If a person's primary protective factor is a belief that suicide is an unforgivable sin, it is unwise and unethical to seek to correct that belief. We can support this understanding, even if we don't agree with it, while trying to help the person add to their protective factors. It is a better choice to deal with the pain, the psychache, of the individual than to worry about a theological belief with which we might not agree. There will be time enough to introduce the person to the concept of God's unconditional love when other protective factors are in place and the risk for suicide is less.

To show the complexity of the ethics involved, let's take a moment to consider survivors of suicide loss. The theological view that kept a person from suicide may be a risk factor for a survivor of suicide loss. When a person believes that their loved one is in hell because they died by suicide, there is a much greater chance that the survivor will engage in suicidal behavior or die by suicide. Who wants to think of a loved one alone in hell for all eternity? Contagion can spread if this goes unaddressed. In this situation, it is wiser to talk about God's capacity for love and the possibilities that God's compassion is far greater than God's judgment. After all, God understands human suffering.

Again, this does not have to match our own theology. Surely we can all entertain the idea that God's actions are not always as we believe them to be. It is possible that God's mercy is extended to those who die by suicide, just as it is equally possible that God's mercy is not given to those who die by suicide. When we seek to save lives, it is not about us or "right beliefs." It is about instilling enough hope for the conversation to continue.

Each of us needs to explore our own beliefs about suicide. We need to figure out how we can respond morally and ethically so as not to increase anyone's risk for suicide. It's complicated and challenging, and absolutely necessary. It is irresponsible to continue to uphold unexamined beliefs around suicide. Lives are at stake. Is it more important to be "theologically correct" or to save a life? What would Jesus have done?

Funeral Dos and Don'ts (Safe Messaging)

Do:

- List the Suicide Prevention Lifeline number on all printed material: 1-800-273-TALK (8255).

- Name suicide as the cause of death without giving details or glorifying it in any way.

- Speak words of hope for those gathered without guaranteeing freedom from pain, eternal life, etc. God values all life.

- Talk about the individual's strengths to indicate that the person should not be defined by suicide alone; they were more than the mental health issues they struggled with.

- Assure people of God's presence with them, with those who are suicidal, with the one who died by suicide. God's heart breaks when anyone suffers such pain.

Don't:

- Ignore suicide as the cause of death.

- Attribute the death to stress or anything else that adds to the stigma of suicide.

- Condemn the one who died.

- Promise that the person is free from pain and in heaven.

- Speak of suicide as an unforgivable sin.

For more information on safe messaging, see the resources provided by the Suicide Prevention Resource Center - http://www.sprc.org.

What to Say and Not Say to Someone Who Is a Suicide Loss Survivor

What to say:

- "I am so sorry for your loss."

- "How are you feeling?" Or, "It's okay if you feel guilt, or shame, or anger. We can talk about any of those things whenever it might be helpful to you."

- "Are you hurting so much that you think about suicide yourself? If you are, I am not judging you; I just want to help you find a way through the pain."

- Respond to theological statements in ways that will support protective factors (see above).

  — If they believe their loved one is in hell: "While God is not a fan of suicide, do you think it's possible that God's mercy is beyond our understanding? Do you think that God's love and forgiveness might be available to your loved one?"

  — If they believe that their loved one is in heaven: "I don't necessarily want to change your mind or suggest that your loved one isn't free from pain. However, I'm worried that you might be thinking about suicide because you are in so much pain, too. Can we talk more about this?"

- "Where are you finding hope right now?" (Be prepared to continue this conversation, because the person may not be able to find hope anywhere.)

What not to say:

- "Suicide is an unforgivable sin and there's no way your loved one is in heaven."

- "Your loved one is free from pain and is at peace with God."

- "You shouldn't talk about the suicide so much. It's over and you need to move on."

- "That was years ago. You should be over that by now."
- "Only faithless people kill themselves. You have faith, so you'll be fine."

What to Do and Not Do When Youth Experience the Suicide of a Peer

Do:

- Name suicide as the cause of death.
- Provide safe space for kids to gather and express themselves.
- Make sure they all have access to the Lifeline number 1-800-273-TALK (8255) and any other local support numbers.
- Identify youth who are at highest risk for contagion and assist in putting extra supports in place: a therapist, social worker, or other therapeutic supports—including caring, knowledgeable adults (such as a pastor, teacher, or coach) who can check in with the individual(s) on a regular basis.
- Be careful and attentive to theological statements that indicate greater risk.
- Stress that suicide is avoidable, explain that anyone who is struggling with thoughts of suicide can be helped, and encourage them to seek help from a responsible adult.
- Remind the youth that telling an adult if one of their peers talks about suicide is not breaking confidence, it's saving a life. It's better to have someone alive and angry at you than to have them die and leave you feeling responsible.

Don't:

- Hold the memorial service in the school.
- Let memorials made of mementoes or gifts stay in place for more than a few days, especially if it has been created on school grounds.
- Discuss any of the specifics of the suicide.
- Make blanket statements about suicide as a sin, *or* about the person being at peace.

- Impose your needs on the youth as they process the loss.

- Say anything that reinforces the stigma around suicide.

- Say anything that glorifies or glamorizes suicide.

How to Make Your Church a Lifesaving Church

- Educate yourself and your congregation on mental illness and suicide.

- Know the resources in your area and make sure they are available to congregants.

- Have a "Mental Health Awareness Sunday" at least once a year.

- Provide space for a Survivors of Suicide Loss support group.

- Provide space for a mental health peer support group.

- Encourage people to talk openly about their mental health challenges.

- Encourage prayer requests about mental health issues, including suicidality and self-harm.

- Respond to mental health crises the same way you respond to physical health crises (e.g., bring meals to family, offer other supports for the family as needed, hold them up in prayer, make pastoral visits, encourage other congregational care visitors, etc.).

- Be a leader in breaking the stigma around suicide and mental illness.

- Find out what your denomination does to support awareness and participate in mental health initiatives.

- Offer support and care to anyone struggling with suicidality, self-harm, or other forms of mental illness.

Resources for Laypeople

Suicide Prevention

As stated in the Epilogue, we work toward the day when all suicides are preventable. Suicide prevention begins with education. It's important to educate yourself on the signs and symptoms of suicide risk. (See Appendix A.) Just as important is to know the resources in your area so that when you encounter someone who is at risk for suicide, you know where they can find help. For your convenience, you can list their specific names and phone numbers here:

- Community Mental Health Clinic:

  _____

- Local Suicide or Mental Health Crisis Hotline:

  _____

- Local Mental Health Provider for Youth:

  _____

- Local Mental Health Provider for LGBTQ+ Youth:

  _____

- Local Mental Health Provider for Adults:

  _____

- Local Mental Health Provider for Seniors:

  _____

- Local National Alliance on Mental Illness (NAMI) Contact: _____

Mostly, suicide prevention is about demythologizing suicide itself. The more we know and the more comfortable we are with talking about it, the more lives that will be saved. At one point or another, many of us have considered suicide, some more actively than others. We all know pain and how easily pain can consume us. This is not a mystery. Suicide becomes an option for a person when they cannot see an end to the pain.

As Christians, we must be agents of hope. I firmly believe that as long as there is breath, there is hope: There is hope for the right medication to be found to ease the depression. There is hope that the right therapist will be found to help find a way through the psychache. There is hope for God's light to shine through the deepest despair. But if we aren't talking about these things, hope becomes nearly impossible to find. Do not be afraid to ask someone you believe to be at risk whether they are indeed thinking about suicide. You will not be increasing the likelihood of suicide by asking the question.

Suicide Intervention

If you think someone is at risk for suicide, don't dismiss that thought. If someone is at imminent risk (e.g., has a plan and means to carry it out and is contacting you to say goodbye), call 9-1-1. If someone tells you that they are thinking of suicide, ask if they have talked to a therapist or any other mental health professional. Validate the feelings they express and affirm how much they mean to you. Say something like, "I understand that you are in pain (or feel hopeless or worthless), and I don't want you to keep feeling this way. I value our friendship and I would like to help." If a person has a therapist, verify that they have shared thoughts of suicide with that person and encourage them to keep doing so. If you are able to listen without judgment, that is also good. Keep affirming the person and encouraging them to find alternatives to suicide to decrease the pain they feel. You may need to check in with a professional to verify you are providing healthy support for the individual. It's important for you to know your limits, and to take care of yourself.

Suicide "Postvention"

The aftermath of suicide can be incredibly painful and overwhelming for family, friends, church community, and the wider community. It's important to be able to speak openly about the suicide and your feelings. It is unwise to discuss in public or private the details or means of suicide. If you find that you have the need to discuss these details, please do so with a qualified professional. With the exception of discussing the means of suicide, talking openly and honestly about a suicide reduces stigma and may minimize contagion (meaning: copycat behavior).

Try your best to respond to survivors of suicide loss the way you would respond to survivors of other types of death. If you would bring a meal to the family, do the same with suicide. If you would send a card or offer any other supports at the time of death, please do so with suicide. The goal is to remove the stigma and shame survivors may feel. When someone loses a loved one to suicide, it is essential to remind them that they are part of wider community and are loved. There is no greater pain than when a parent loses a child to suicide. That pain will never end, though with time and support, the pain diminishes or at least takes on a shape that is bearable. We should never expect any suicide loss survivors to "get over" the loss. The grief is complicated and often without end. Be patient. Be willing to listen. Be an agent of hope simply by showing up and being willing to share the journey for a while.

Resources for Those Struggling with Suicidality

This list is meant as a place to begin or continue finding hope and support. It is not meant to be a comprehensive list. If you are planning to die by suicide, please call the Suicide Prevention Lifeline (listed below) or go to your nearest emergency room. If you think of suicide often, please look through these resources, consider sharing your thoughts with someone you trust, and seek professional help. You are not alone in your pain and there is hope for you. Please reach out for help.

Suicide Prevention Lifeline: 1-800-273-TALK (8255)

- Crisis Chat is a service of the National Suicide Prevention Lifeline. Here you can chat live without having to make a phone call, if chatting online is easier for you.

  http://www.crisischat.org/

For Veterans:
- Life Line for Veterans is a branch of the National Suicide Prevention Lifeline for veterans. Call: 1-800-273-8255 and Press 1; Text to 838255; or Chat online 24/7/365.

  https://www.veteranscrisisline.net/

For Youth:
- You Matter is for youth between the ages of 13 and 24. It is a safe space for sharing and supporting one another. It is monitored by the National Suicide Prevention Lifeline.

  http://youmatter.suicidepreventionlifeline.org/

- Active Minds is a nonprofit organization for college-age people. The organization's goal is to change the conversation around mental illness through education, understanding, and support.

  http://activeminds.org/

- Love Is Respect offers information and support for young people who have experienced relationship violence.

  http://www.loveisrespect.org

- Ditch the Label is an excellent anti-bullying resource. It offers a wide variety of support and information for those who experience bullying and those who have been bullies.

  https://us.ditchthelabel

- The Jed Foundation focuses on suicide prevention and mental health for teens and young adults.

  https://www.jedfoundation

For LGBTQ+ Youth:
- The Trevor Project is a national organization that provides suicide prevention and crisis intervention for LGBTQ+ people ages 13–24.

  http://www.thetrevorproject.org/

- It Gets Better focuses primarily on offering information and support to LGBTQ+ youth. (This might not be helpful in an immediate crisis situation.)

  http://www.itgetsbetter.org/

Appendix E

Resources for Suicide Loss Survivors

This is a list of a few online resources. Sometimes online is a helpful place to start when grieving someone who died by suicide. If it has been many months or years since your loss and you are still overwhelmed by grief, please seek professional help. Many cities and towns have support groups for suicide loss survivors. Individual grief counseling with someone who understands the complexities of suicide loss may also be helpful. You are not alone and you do not need to endure grief on your own. Please reach out for help.

- American Foundation for Suicide Prevention is a national organization. The "Find Support" section on this site has good information and resources for survivors of suicide loss.

  https://afsp.org/

- Suicide Grief Support Forum is an interactive site that is not meant for crisis situations. However, sharing the stories of others who have survived suicide loss may provide hope.

  http://www.suicidegrief.com/

- The Alliance of Hope for Suicide Loss Survivors is a nonprofit organization that seeks to offer support and hope to survivors of suicide loss. http://www.allianceofhope.org/

- Compassionate Friends is a national organization that offers support and resources for those who've lost a loved one to sudden, violent death.

  https://www.compassionatefriends.org/

- The Connect Program is based in New Hampshire, but has good, broad-based, accessible information for suicide loss survivors.

  http://www.theconnectprogram.org/

- The National Alliance for Mental Illness (NAMI) is a national organization offering information and support for those living with or caring for those who live with mental illness. Most states have a NAMI chapter that offers support in local communities. This is also a good resource for those at risk for suicide.

  http://www.nami.org/

- Suicide Awareness Voices of Education (SAVE) provides resources for Suicide Loss Survivors, including the oldest and longest running suicide memorial (SAVE also has resources for those struggling with suicidality).

  https://save.org

For Postvention:
- This is a link to the Postvention Manual complied by the Suicide Prevention Resource Center (SPRC).

  http://www.sprc.org/sites/default/files/migrate/library/LifelineOnlinePostventionManual.pdf

Scripture Verses and Stories That Emphasize Hope

Psalm 139:1-18

O Lord, you have searched me and known me. You know
when I sit down and when I rise up;
you discern my thoughts from far away.
You search out my path and my lying down,
and are acquainted with all my ways.
Even before a word is on my tongue,
O Lord, you know it completely.
You hem me in, behind and before,
and lay your hand upon me.
Such knowledge is too wonderful for me;
it is so high that I cannot attain it.

Where can I go from your spirit?
Or where can I flee from your presence?
If I ascend to heaven, you are there;
if I make my bed in Sheol, you are there.
If I take the wings of the morning
and settle at the farthest limits of the sea,
even there your hand shall lead me,
and your right hand shall hold me fast.
If I say, "Surely the darkness shall cover me,
and the light around me become night,"
even the darkness is not dark to you;
the night is as bright as the day,
for darkness is as light to you.

For it was you who formed my inward parts;
you knit me together in my mother's womb.
I praise you, for I am fearfully and wonderfully made.
Wonderful are your works;
that I know very well.
My frame was not hidden from you,
when I was being made in secret,
intricately woven in the depths of the earth.
Your eyes beheld my unformed substance.
In your book were written
all the days that were formed for me,
when none of them as yet existed.
How weighty to me are your thoughts, O God!
How vast is the sum of them!
I try to count them—they are more than the sand;
I come to the end—I am still with you.

Isaiah 41:10

[D]o not fear, for I am with you,
do not be afraid, for I am your God;
I will strengthen you, I will help you,
I will uphold you with my victorious right hand.

Isaiah 43:1–5a

But now thus says the LORD,
he who created you, O Jacob,
he who formed you, O Israel:
Do not fear, for I have redeemed you;
I have called you by name, you are mine.
When you pass through the waters, I will be with you;
and through the rivers, they shall not overwhelm you;
when you walk through fire you shall not be burned,
and the flame shall not consume you.
For I am the LORD your God,
the Holy One of Israel, your Savior.
I give Egypt as your ransom,
Ethiopia and Seba in exchange for you.
Because you are precious in my sight,
and honored, and I love you,

I give people in return for you,
nations in exchange for your life.
Do not fear, for I am with you...

Jeremiah 29:11

For surely I know the plans I have for you, says the LORD,
plans for your welfare and not for harm, to give you a
future with hope.

Matthew 11:28–30

[Jesus said,] "Come to me, all you that are weary and are
carrying heavy burdens, and I will give you rest. Take my
yoke upon you, and learn from me; for I am gentle and
humble in heart, and you will find rest for your souls. For
my yoke is easy, and my burden is light."

John 14:26–27

[Jesus said,] "But the Advocate, the Holy Spirit, whom the
Father will send in my name, will teach you everything,
and remind you of all that I have said to you. Peace I
leave with you; my peace I give to you. I do not give to
you as the world gives. Do not let your hearts be troubled,
and do not let them be afraid."

Romans 8:38–39

For I am convinced that neither death, nor life, nor
angels, nor rulers, nor things present, nor things to come,
nor powers, nor height, nor depth, nor anything else in
all creation, will be able to separate us from the love of
God in Christ Jesus our Lord.

Romans 15:13

May the God of hope fill you with all joy and peace in
believing, so that you may abound in hope by the power
of the Holy Spirit.

Also consider: the story of Rahab (Josh. 2), the woman caught
in adultery (Jn. 7:53—8:11), the Samaritan woman at the well
(Jn. 4), and the man born blind (Jn. 9). Rahab was a prostitute

who, through her actions, made it into Matthew's genealogy of Jesus. The woman caught in adultery was not condemned; she was forgiven and sent on her way. The Samaritan woman was not condemned for her past choices and was transformed into one of the first evangelists. Jesus gave sight to the man born blind when most saw him as nothing more than a sinner. More importantly, Jesus did this so that all could see the glory of God manifest in the one who had been dismissed as a blind beggar.

Prayers

For One Struggling with Suicidality or Self-Harm

Holy God, I am not sure where you are, or even *if* you are. I am feeling lost, and the pain I feel seems overwhelming and never-ending. I want to believe your promise of new life. I want to believe the Good News Jesus preached. I want to be a part of the fullness of your realm here on earth. But right now, it is too hard. You seem too far away.

Jesus, you know what pain and suffering feel like. Be with me. Wrap me in your love. Better still, place someone in my path who will show me how much I am loved and valued. It's so hard to see that my life matters. I want to believe that you gave me this gift of life. I want to believe that this pain will end and healing will come.

Show me the way of your love. Help me to reach out and trust those around me so they can hold hope for me while I cannot hold any for myself. Let me believe them when they tell me they want me to live. Open my heart to the path for healing even as you ease this pain I carry. Give me a spirit of willingness and enough patience to pursue wholeness and not give up. Let me see my own worth and your great love for me. I don't want to feel so alone. Wrap me in your grace and get me through this painful darkness.

Fill me with the power of your forgiveness and love so that I may walk in the light of your love.

I pray in the name of Jesus who came to seek and to save the lost, Amen.

For a Survivor of Suicide Loss

God, I am so angry and sad right now that I'm not even sure I want to talk to you. How could you let such a thing happen? How could I? I've never felt such pain and guilt and sadness all mixed together. People tell me how sorry they are, but they want me to be over the loss and get on with my life. I don't know when or if that will ever happen.

Please, take this pain from me. I want to believe that [*name of the departed*] is with you, at peace in your presence and free from all that was overwhelming in this life. I want to believe that you are here with me now, that I am not alone as I try to make sense out of this senseless death. By the power of your love, take away the shame and guilt I feel.

Stay with me, Jesus. Walk with me through this grief. You called Lazarus out of his tomb and gave him new life. Call me out of this pit of despair. I cannot go back to the life I had before this happened. You must lead me to new life, even though I cannot imagine it.

Grant me the courage to face the challenges of each day. When the tears flow, be with me. When the anger rips through me, be with me. Whisper words of love and hope and forgiveness until I am able to hear them.

Wrap me in your steadfast love now and always.

In the name of the One who conquered sin and death, Amen.

For Congregations When a Member Has Died by Suicide

Holy God, hear our prayers for the family and friends of [*name of the departed*]. We feel this loss and recognize again how vulnerable the Body of Christ truly is. While we feel anger, guilt, shame, and sadness, remind us anew that we are yours. You understand how the body can break and then come together again in an unimagined wholeness. Just as you offered your broken body for forgiveness and life, may we embody this same forgiveness and this same life for all those we encounter.

Guide us through this loss and shape us into a community that is fearless when it comes to grace. Let us be a sanctuary for those who struggle with suicidality and self-harm. May all those who come through our doors trust us with their feelings of worthlessness or pain, as well as any other mental health challenges. Teach us how to be a community of love and hope.

As we seek to embody you, O Christ, let the life and death of [*name of the departed*] have meaning. May we learn from the mistakes of our past to create a future filled with hope. Break the remaining silences here so that no one must suffer alone. Stigma has no place in your church. We are the Body of Christ. May we truly be about saving lives from this moment forward.

Forgive us. Strengthen us. Heal us. Make us whole.

We pray in the name of Jesus, who came to show us how to love with your love. Amen.